YA 5361701K
303.625 Innes, Brian.
INN International
terrorism

SEQUOYAH REGIONAL LIBRARY SYST

S0-CTY-781

ROSE CREEK PUBLIC LIBRARY
4476 TOWNE LAKE PKWY.
WOODSTOCK, GA 30189

SEQUOYAH REGIONAL LIBRARY

3 8749 0053 6170 1

CRIME AND DETECTION

INTERNATIONAL TERRORISM

> DEDICATION
>
> This book is dedicated to those who perished in the terrorist attacks of September 11, 2001, and to all the committed individuals who continually serve to defend freedom and protect the American people.

Crime and Detection series

- Criminal Terminology
- Cyber Crime
- Daily Prison Life
- Death Row and Capital Punishment
- Domestic Crime
- Famous Prisons
- Famous Trials
- Forensic Science
- Government Intelligence Agencies
- Hate Crimes
- The History and Methods of Torture
- The History of Punishment
- International Terrorism
- Major Unsolved Crimes
- Organized Crime
- Protecting Yourself Against Criminals
- Race and Crime
- Serial Murders
- The United States Justice System
- The War Against Drugs

CRIME AND DETECTION

INTERNATIONAL TERRORISM

BRIAN INNES

PROPERTY OF
THE SEQUOYAH REGIONAL
LIBRARY SYSTEM CANTON, GA.

MASON CREST PUBLISHERS
www.masoncrest.com

Mason Crest Publishers Inc.
370 Reed Road
Broomall, PA 19008
(866) MCP-BOOK (toll free)
www.masoncrest.com

Copyright © 2004 Mason Crest Publishers.

All rights reserved. No part of this publication may be reproduced or transmitted in any form or by any means, electronic or mechanical, including photocopying, recording, taping, or any information storage and retrieval system, without permission in writing from the publisher.

2 3 4 5 6 7 8 9 10

Innes, Brian.
 International terrorism / Brian Innes.
   v. cm. -- (Crime and detection)
Includes bibliographical references and index.
Contents: Introduction -- The rise of terrorism -- The rise of the PLO -- Urban guerrillas -- Terrorism and religion -- Osama bin Laden and al Qaeda -- Counter-terrorist organizations.
 ISBN 1-59084-371-1
 1. Terrorism--Juvenile literature. 2. Terrorists--Juvenile literature. [1. Terrorism. 2. Terrorists.] I. Title. II. Series

 HV6431.I5563 2003
 303.6'25--dc21   2003000485

Editorial and design by
Amber Books Ltd.
Bradley's Close
74–77 White Lion Street
London N1 9PF
www.amberbooks.co.uk

Project Editor: Michael Spilling
Design: Floyd Sayers
Picture Research: Natasha Jones

Printed and bound in Malaysia

Picture credits
Mary Evans Picture Library: 12; PA Photos: 73; Popperfoto: 30, 46, 81, 88; Topham Picturepoint: 6, 8, 11, 13, 16–17, 19, 20, 23, 24, 27, 29, 32, 33, 34, 36, 39, 40, 41, 43, 48, 51, 52, 55, 57, 58, 60, 61, 65, 67, 68, 70, 74, 77, 82–83, 84, 87; TRH: 89; U.S. Department of Defense: 78.
Front cover: Topham Picturepoint.

CONTENTS

Introduction	7
The Rise of Terrorism	9
The Rise of the PLO	25
Urban Guerrillas	35
Terrorism and Religion	53
Osama bin Laden and Al Qaeda	71
Counterterrorist Organizations	85
Glossary	90
Chronology	92
Further Information	94
Index	96

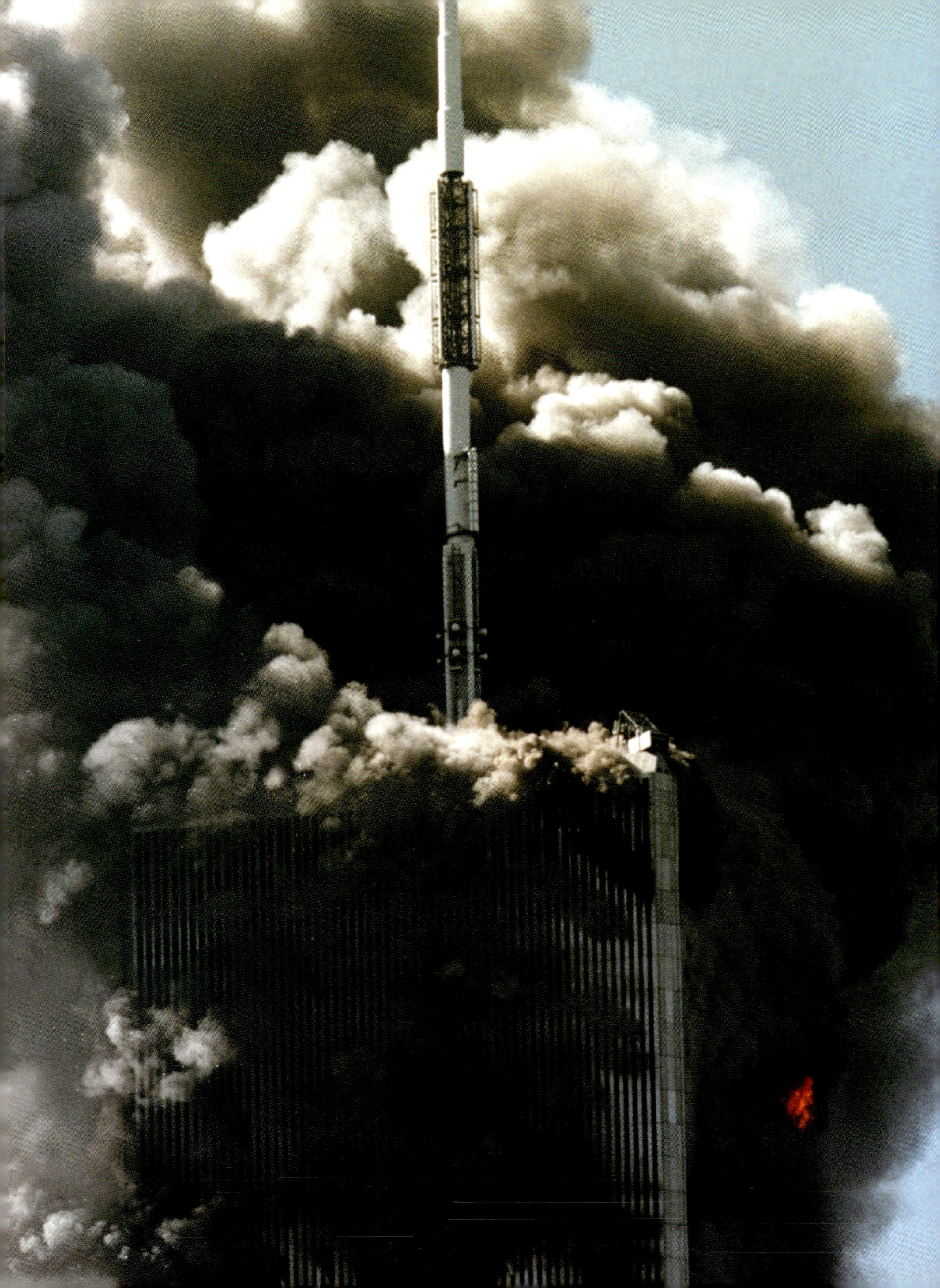

Introduction

From the moment in the Book of Genesis when Cain's envy of his brother Abel erupted into violence, crime has been an inescapable feature of human life. Every society ever known has had its own sense of how things ought to be, its deeply held views on how men and women should behave. Yet in every age there have been individuals ready to break these rules for their own advantage: they must be resisted if the community is to thrive.

This exciting and vividly illustrated new series sets out the history of crime and detection from the earliest times to the present day, from the empires of the ancient world to the towns and cities of the 21st century. From the commandments of the great religions to the theories of modern psychologists, it considers changing attitudes toward offenders and their actions. Contemporary crime is examined in its many different forms: everything from racial hatred to industrial espionage, from serial murder to drug trafficking, from international terrorism to domestic violence.

The series looks, too, at the work of those men and women entrusted with the task of overseeing and maintaining the law, from judges and court officials to police officers and other law enforcement agents. The tools and techniques at their disposal are described and vividly illustrated, and the ethical issues they face concisely and clearly explained.

All in all, the *Crime and Detection* series provides a comprehensive and accessible account of crime and detection, in theory and in practice, past and present.

CHARLIE FULLER

Executive Director, International Association of Undercover Officers

Left: Smoke billows from one of the Twin Towers of the World Trade Center in New York City, following the terrorist suicide bombings on the morning of September 11, 2001. More than 3,000 people were killed as a result of the attacks in New York City and on the Pentagon.

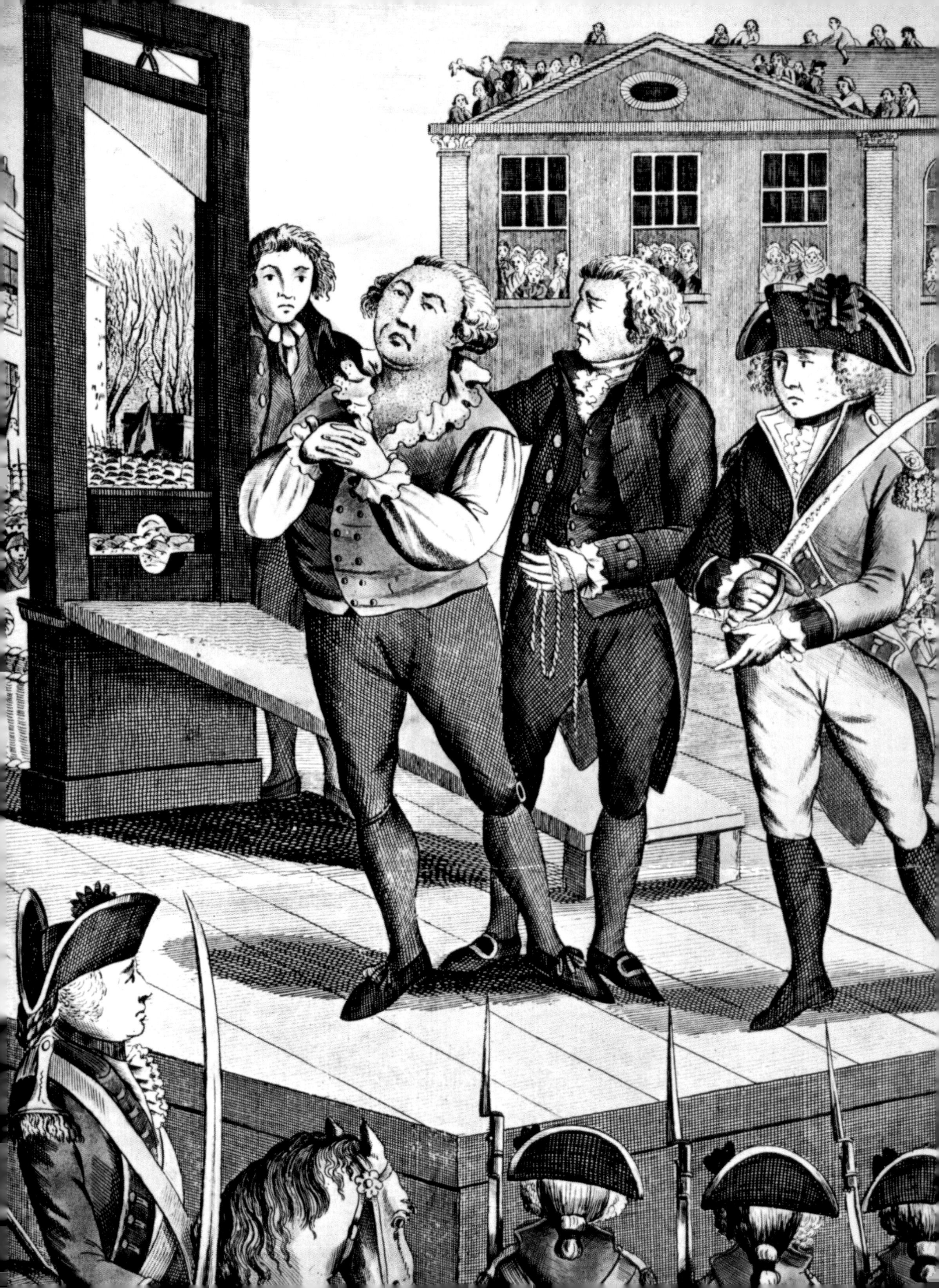

The Rise of Terrorism

The word "terrorist" is, sadly, one that has become increasingly familiar around the world in recent years. It is, however, some two centuries old, and originally had a different meaning. It was first used to describe the "terror" of the years 1793-1794, following the French Revolution of 1789. This was a time of upheaval, and the new government had to find a way of suppressing the "enemies of the people." The Committee of General Security and the Revolutionary Tribunal were given wide-ranging powers of arrest and judgment, and anybody found guilty of treason (antigovernment activity) was put to death on the guillotine. One of the first people to die was King Louis XVI, who went to the scaffold in January 1793. Many others followed (an estimated 40,000), unhappy victims of the "terrorists."

DEFINING TERRORISM

Terrorism was seen at that time as a way of protecting democracy. As the revolutionary leader Maximilien Robespierre put it: "Terror is nothing but justice, prompt, severe, and inflexible; it is therefore an emanation of virtue." However, the pursuit of "traitors" gradually got out of hand. In July 1794, Robespierre announced that he held a new list of those suspected of treasonable offenses. There were many who were fearful that their names were on the list, and they joined forces to suppress the "terror."

As a result, Robespierre and his close associates went to the guillotine, and terrorism became a word associated with the abuse of power. English politician Edmund Burke spoke of "thousands of those hellhounds called

Left: The origins of the word "terrorism" came in the years of terror that followed the French Revolution of 1789. By order of the Committee of General Security, anyone suspected of treason—including the imprisoned king Louis XVI—was sentenced to be beheaded by guillotine.

Terrorists…let loose upon the people." The example of the French Revolution sparked off a wave of revolts against the rule of kings in Europe. In 1848, the "year of revolution," there were popular uprisings in Italy, France, Austria, Poland, and other countries, all demanding changes in their constitutions and the establishment of the rights of common people. One of the most active **republicans** in Italy was Carlo Pisacane, who gave up his title of Duke of San Giovanni. He put forward the doctrine of "propaganda by deed," arguing that violence was necessary, not only to attract publicity to revolt, but also to educate the masses and gain their support. Pisacane's theory has become the justification behind modern terrorism: as it has been expressed recently, "one man's terrorist is another man's freedom fighter."

THE ANARCHISTS

One of the first movements to put Pisacane's principles into practice was the *Narodnaya Volya* (People's Will), founded in Russia in 1878 to oppose the rule of the **czar**. Unlike modern-day terrorist organizations, however, they carefully selected individual targets, such as the czar and members of his family or senior members of the government, and maintained that "not one drop of superfluous blood should be shed." A good example of this was the planned attempt on the life of Grand Duke Serge Alexandrovich in 1905. When the terrorist assigned to the assassination saw that the duke's children were with him in his carriage, he immediately gave up the attempt.

By that date, the *Narodnaya Volya* had been almost wiped out following their assassination of Czar Alexander II on March 1, 1881. The first terrorist hurled his bomb at the czar's sleigh. It missed, and soldiers seized the terrorist. As Alexander stepped from the sleigh, remarking, "Thank God, I am safe," a second man sprang from the crowd with another bomb and killed both the czar and himself. Brutal interrogation of the surviving terrorist soon provided enough information to round up the members of the organization, who were convicted and hanged.

THE RISE OF TERRORISM 11

The body of the Russian Czar Alexander II, lying in state before his funeral in 1881. Two bombers from the revolutionary movement Narodnaya Volya attacked his sleigh, close by the Winter Palace, as it passed through the streets of St Petersburg.

Plotting against czarist rule nevertheless continued. There were many secret societies formed, both in Russia and abroad. The Russians gave them the general name of *narodniks*; in Western Europe, they were known as "**anarchists**." Many of the bombers were connected to political parties, such as the Communist Party, which sought to overthrow the old order throughout Europe. Shortly after the czar's assassination, an "anarchist conference" was held in London, at which the establishment of an Anarchist—or "Black"—International was announced. Anarchists were judged responsible for a dramatic number of bombings and other killings that took place well into the 20th century. On September 6, 1901, U.S. President William McKinley was shot dead by a young Hungarian, Leon

A CARTOON ANARCHIST

Despite the real threat they posed, the anarchists became a favorite target for humorists, as in this illustration from the French magazine *Le Rire* of 1903. As late as the 1930s, "Bombski," in his black hat and long cloak, and holding a smoldering bomb, was a popular comic-strip character in a British newspaper.

THE RISE OF TERRORISM   13

Czolgocz. Congress at once passed legislation barring known anarchists—or anyone "who disbelieves in or is opposed to all organized government"—from entering the U.S.

Gavrilo Princip, an anarchist, was responsible for initiating a series of events that led to World War I. Bosnian Serbs had been agitating for independence from the Austro-Hungarian empire, and in 1911, the secret organization *Udejinjenje ili Smrt* (Unity or Death) was formed; popularly, it was known as the "Black Hand." Princip, trained by the Black Hand, shot Archduke Ferdinand and his wife on June 28, 1914, in Sarajevo. Germany backed Austro-Hungary in its retaliation on Serbia, and took

Seconds after the fatal pistol attack upon the Austrian Archduke Ferdinand and his wife on June 28, 1914, Gavrilo Princip is hustled away by guards and bystanders. This incident in Sarajevo, intended only as a blow struck for the independence of Bosnian Serbs, led to World War I.

advantage of the tense situation to attack both France and Russia a month later. Britain, Italy, Japan, Canada, Australia, New Zealand, and eventually the U.S. were among the countries drawn into the conflict—World War I—which lasted four years and killed millions.

THE IRISH REPUBLICAN ARMY

For more than a century before World War I, the majority of the people of Ireland had been seeking independence from the United Kingdom. In Northern Ireland, however, there was a fiercely loyalist majority, which was opposed to any break with Britain. The problem was directly connected with religion. The original Irish adhered to Roman Catholicism, a faith that was not legalized in Britain until 1829, after three centuries of the Churches of England and Scotland. The predominant northerners were descendants of Protestant Scots, settled there since 1609 and, particularly, since the defeat of the deposed Catholic king of Britain, James II, in 1690.

On Easter 1917, with minor support from the Germans, the Irish Republican Brotherhood rose in rebellion in Dublin (although the Germans had previously supplied 35,000 rifles to the northern **Ulster** Volunteers). The British government soon put down the revolution, and its leaders were all executed by firing squad. However, it gained overwhelming support for its political party, Sinn Fein, in the subsequent southern elections. The survivors went on the run, and one, Michael Collins, was responsible for the formation of the Irish Republican Army (IRA), which soon began a **guerrilla** war against the British occupation.

In 1921, the British offered independence to southern Ireland, but insisted on keeping four Protestant counties of the northern province of Ulster in the U.K. Collins accepted the agreement, but his rival leader, Eamonn de Valera, and a majority of the IRA, rejected it. Civil war broke out between the two, Collins was assassinated, and a **cease-fire** was not signed until May 1923. The Irish Free State was renamed Eire in 1937 and the Republic of Ireland in 1949.

THE MAFIA

What has become the world's most widespread criminal organization—known variously as the Mafia, Cosa Nostra, the Syndicate, or more loosely "the Mob"—began life as a Sicilian secret society whose terrorism was directed at rich landlords.

The Mafia has long imposed a code known as *omertà* (silence) on their members: never to seek justice from legal authorities and never to assist criminal investigations in any way. Vengeance for violence committed against a person is reserved to the victim or members of his family. The Mafia initially controlled the employment of workers on the big estates and operated protection rackets. When Sicilian immigrants began to arrive in the United States toward the end of the 19th century, some organized themselves in a similar way.

In Italy, when the fascist dictator Benito Mussolini came to power in 1925, he had many Mafia leaders imprisoned for life. Unfortunately, when U.S. forces landed in Sicily in 1943, these men were released as "antifascists," and some were even set up as mayors and local government officials. In this way, the Mafia was returned to power in the island and, despite many efforts by the Italian authorities, they continue their reign of terrorism and maintain criminal contacts throughout the world.

AN UNSATISFACTORY SOLUTION

However, many people still desired a complete unification of Ireland, and surviving members of the IRA continued terrorist attacks against the British authorities, even after de Valera outlawed them in 1936. By 1962, however, the IRA was unwilling to be involved in the sectarian conflict in Northern Ireland and declared a cease-fire. Meanwhile, an active civil rights

16 INTERNATIONAL TERRORISM

movement had developed, demanding equality for Catholics in housing, work, and electoral status. The illegal Protestant Ulster Volunteer Force began to terrorize Catholic residents of Belfast in 1966, and, when Protestants attacked a civil rights march in 1969, a new "Provisional" IRA (soon known as the "Provos," but identified by many as the original IRA) was formed in retaliation. The British Army was called in to restore order, the Northern Ireland government was suspended, and terrorism broke out again on both sides.

THE RISE OF TERRORISM 17

The Provos' campaign intensified during the 1970s, with repeated bombings in England and attacks on Protestants in Northern Ireland. In 1979, they assassinated Earl Mountbatten, an uncle of Queen Elizabeth, and three others; and in 1989, they began a series of bombing attacks on British bases in West Germany.

In 1998, however, the Good Friday agreement was signed. The Provos announced a cease-fire, and the Sinn Fein political party was officially recognized. Nevertheless, hard-liners formed the "Real IRA," and terrorist violence between Catholics and Protestants continues in Northern Ireland.

In Northern Ireland, Protestant concern about projected reforms that would give equal social status to Catholics, gave rise to the formation of a number of illegal terrorist organizations, such as the Ulster Volunteer Force, which renewed sectarian violence in the province from 1966 onward.

STATE TERRORISM RETURNS

During the 1930s and 1940s, "terror" once again meant the use of violence by governments against their citizens. **Fascist** regimes in Spain, Italy, and Germany ruthlessly suppressed all "enemies of the state," such as political opponents, Communists, Jews, and others. (Ironically, the activities of the French Resistance during the German occupation of France—including the derailment of trains and the assassination of German soldiers in the streets and of those suspected of collaboration with the occupying forces—were hailed as acts of heroism, but not by the Germans.) In Russia, Stalin's "Great Terror" eliminated all those who challenged his absolute power, as well as many others who did not toe the party line.

Even in the 1970s through the 1990s, military dictatorships in Argentina, Chile, and Greece, as well as elected governments in El Salvador, Guatemala, Colombia, and Peru, took similar measures against political opponents, human-rights workers, students, labor organizers, and journalists. State terrorism remains a danger, but the current spread of international terrorism is of even greater concern.

THE TERRORIST NETWORK

Following the end of World War II in 1945, most terrorist organizations that emerged were devoted to throwing off colonial rule and achieving national independence. This was particularly true in much of the British empire or areas under British control: in the Near East, Africa, and Southeastern Asia. Two of the most notorious were Jewish movements in Palestine: the Irgun (National Military Organization), led by the future prime minister of Israel, Menachem Begin; and the Stern Gang (so-named after its founder, Abraham Stern), whose chosen name was "Freedom Fighters for Israel." In May 1946, Irgun blew up part of the King David Hotel in Jerusalem, which contained British government and military offices, leading to 91 deaths. How much their activities contributed to the establishment of the state of Israel two years later is, however, debatable.

THE RISE OF TERRORISM   **19**

A "Wanted" poster for the leading members of the Stern Gang, circulated in Jerusalem in 1946.
A photograph of Abraham Stern, the founder of the terrorist organization, is at upper right.

Heavily masked to prevent identification, and with their weapons laid out on the table before them to indicate their serious intent, members of the Basque separatist organization ETA hold a clandestine press conference in February 1982. Here, they announce that they are about to renew their armed conflict with the Spanish government.

The Stern Gang was the last such movement to accept being described as terrorists. Since then, terrorist organizations have given themselves names that include such praiseworthy words as "liberation," "freedom," or "defense," or neutral-sounding titles, like "Shining Path."

Declaring themselves to be soldiers—but wearing no recognized uniform—terrorists claim they are entitled, if captured, to be treated as prisoners of war and not prosecuted as criminals in civil court. However, there are a series of international agreements—the Geneva and Hague Conventions on Warfare (1864, 1899, 1907, and 1949)—that terrorists regularly ignore. These conventions grant civilians immunity from attack;

prohibit taking civilians as hostages; outlaw reprisals; recognize the rights of neutral states; and insist on the safety of diplomats and other accredited persons. Over the past 25 years, terrorist groups have broken all these rules.

Particularly notable has been the violation of those parts of the international conventions that deal with the rights of neutral states and their civilian populations. Terrorists, with few exceptions, do not limit their activities to attacks on oppressive governments or occupying powers. Indiscriminate violence is now the signature of international terrorism.

ETA

One of the most dangerous modern nationalist terrorist organizations is active in Spain. This is the Basque separatist movement *Euskadi Ta Askatasuna* (ETA). In the Basque language, which is known as Euskera, this means "Basque Homeland and Freedom."

The government of Spain officially recognizes three Basque provinces in the northern part of the country, but separatists claim not only the neighboring province of Navarra, but also three districts in southwestern France as Basque country. For centuries, the Basques in Spain enjoyed a fair degree of independence, but under Franco's fascist dictatorship, from 1939

WHAT FASCIST LEADERS SAID

"Terror?" inquired Italian dictator Benito Mussolini. "Never, simply social hygiene, taking those individuals out of circulation like a doctor would take out a bacillus [bacterium]."

In Germany, the new Nazi minister for the interior, Hermann Goering, declared in 1933: "My measures will not be crippled by any judicial thinking. My measures will not be crippled by any bureaucracy. Here, I don't have to worry about Justice; my mission is only to destroy and exterminate, nothing more."

through 1975, they were suppressed and even their language was forbidden.

ETA was founded in 1959 and, with the death of Franco and the return of democracy to Spain, they hoped to achieve recognition of Euskadi as a separate European state. When this hope was not realized, they began a campaign of violence against the Spanish government in 1968. They have targeted politicians, police, judges, and the military—but their principal weapons, car bombs, have also caused hundreds of civilian casualties. ETA has been responsible for more than 800 deaths and 70 kidnappings. In 1980 alone, they killed 118 people, and in 1995, they nearly succeeded in assassinating Jose Aznar, who is currently prime minister of Spain.

According to the U.S. State Department, ETA activists have received training in Libya, Lebanon, and Nicaragua. They also maintained close links with the Provisional IRA in Northern Ireland. When the 1998 Good Friday agreement led to a cease-fire there, they followed suit, declaring a

WE ARE NOT TERRORISTS!

Terry Anderson was an American journalist held hostage for nearly seven years by the Lebanese terrorist organization, Hizballah. One of his guards objected bitterly to a newspaper article: "We are not terrorists," he exclaimed. "We are fighters." Anderson told him: "Look it up in the dictionary. You are a terrorist, you may not like the word, and if you do not like the word, do not do it."

The spiritual leader of the Hizballah, Sheikh Muhammad Hussein Fadlallah, went further in his book, *Invisible Armies*: "We don't see ourselves as terrorists, because we don't believe in terrorism. We don't see resisting the occupier as a terrorist action. We see ourselves as *mujihadin* (holy warriors) who fight a Holy War for the people."

THE RISE OF TERRORISM 23

A victim of the ETA campaign for Basque independence, Lieutenant Colonel Jose Moreno lies riddled with bullets in a Madrid street in November 1989. After a brief cease-fire in 1998–99, ETA has renewed its terrorist attacks, some involving innocent tourists.

"unilateral and indefinite" cease-fire in Spain. However, this lasted just over 12 months, and the year 2000 saw a rapid escalation of terrorism. In 2001, ETA announced that they would target innocent tourists.

The Spanish government has had only moderate success in cracking down on ETA. In 1980, in an effort to defuse the situation, the Basque provinces were recognized as a self-governing region, with their own parliament and police force, and Euskera as the official language, but ETA terrorism has continued unabated.

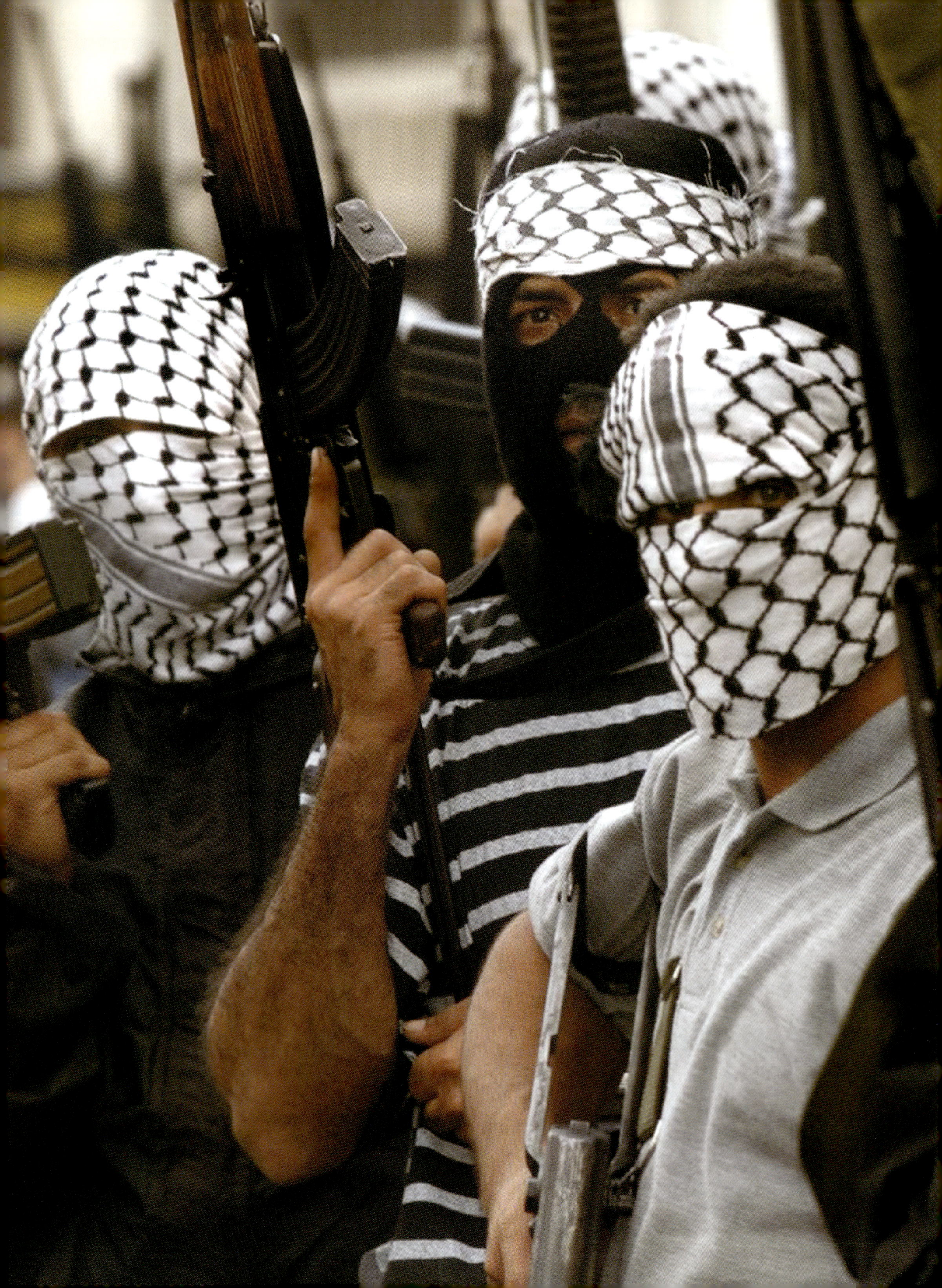

The Rise of the PLO

To understand the current situation, it is important to know a little of the 20th-century history of the area called Palestine. In 1914, the land and its Semitic peoples had been, for centuries, under the control of Turkey, who entered World War I on the side of the Germans and Austro-Hungarians. The Arab inhabitants rose up against the Turks and were encouraged by the British, with the active assistance of T.E. Lawrence—"Lawrence of Arabia." Moreover, Baron Edmond de Rothschild, a rich British scientist, had already begun to encourage Zionist settlement. In 1917, the British government promised him support for a Jewish national home in Palestine—provided that "nothing shall be done which may prejudice the civil and religious rights of existing non-Jewish communities in Palestine."

THE DIVISION OF PALESTINE

After the end of the war, Palestine was divided: Lebanon and Syria were put under French control, and the land to the south was put under British control. In 1927, the area known as Transjordan (now Jordan) was recognized as an independent state, although it remained under British supervision until 1946, when it was declared a kingdom. In what remained of Palestine, Jewish immigration increased, and the Arabs became violently opposed to the establishment of a Jewish national home. In 1936, they revolted, and a British inquiry made the first suggestion for the partition of the country into a Zionist and an Arab state—a proposal that was finally approved by the United Nations in 1947.

Left: Masked and armed, Palestinian gunmen march through the West Bank city of Nablus in October 2000. More than 400, reportedly from the al-Fatah movement, began to organize militia groups to defend neighboring villages against possible attacks from Israeli settlers.

On May 14, 1948, the independent state of Israel was declared and recognized by U.S. president Harry S. Truman. The next day, troops from Syria, Jordan, Iraq, and Egypt invaded the new state and occupied substantial parts of the "Holy Land," including Hebron, Bethlehem, and part of the city of Jerusalem. The Israeli forces, however, proved more successful, capturing wide tracts of land and beating off Arab attacks on scattered settlements. A peace treaty was signed in April 1949, but violent unrest—including two further major wars—has continued ever since, exacerbated by increasing Israeli incursions into Arab territory.

At the end of the Arab-Israeli war in 1949, nearly a million Arab refugees from Palestine were crowded into camps in Jordan, Syria, Lebanon, and Egypt, hoping for the time when their Arab brothers would destroy Israel and let them return to their homes. However, the defeated states were in no mood to start another war, and so small commando groups (the *fedayeen*) began to make hit-and-run raids into Israel. By 1953, these attacks, supported in particular by Egypt, caused Israel to mount military reprisals; and the 1956 Suez crisis provided them with the excuse to wipe out Egyptian bases in the Sinai Peninsula. It was not until 1964, however, that, with the encouragement of Egyptian president Gamal Abdel Nasser, the Palestine Liberation Organization (PLO) was founded in Jordan with the purpose of uniting the anti-Israeli groups.

MODERN INTERNATIONAL TERRORISM

The PLO was responsible for the first incident of modern international terrorism. On July 22, 1968, three armed Palestinians of the Popular Front for the Liberation of Palestine (PFLP, a PLO-aligned group) hijacked an Israeli El Al commercial flight en route from Rome to Tel Aviv. Hijacking was not a new phenomenon, but this incident differed from all previous ones. The terrorists were not just attempting to divert the flight to another destination, but were holding the plane and passengers hostage, demanding their exchange for Palestinians imprisoned in Israel. In this way, Israel was forced to negotiate directly with terrorists—a new and significant development. At the same time, their action attracted international attention. "When we hijack a plane, it has more effect than if we killed 100 Israelis in battle," the PFLP founder later stated. "For decades, world opinion has been neither for nor against the Palestinians. It simply ignored us. At least the world is talking about us now."

International terrorism had achieved a new dimension. For the first time, terrorists were traveling from one country to another to make their attacks. And their targets were no longer official representatives of an oppressive power, not even citizens of that power, but innocent civilians from uninvolved countries. The following year, Yasser Arafat was elected chairman of the PLO and the Palestinians began to train terrorists from other countries in their camps in Jordan.

After the Arab-Israeli war in 1949, nearly a million Palestinians found refuge in camps in Jordan, Syria, Lebanon, and Egypt, where training camps were set up for military operations against Israel. These volunteers were photographed during training at a north Lebanon camp in 1993.

A BLACK SEPTEMBER COMMUNIQUE

One week after Munich, Black September published a proud announcement in a Beirut newspaper:

"In our assessment, and in light of the result, we have made one of the best achievements of Palestinian commando action. A bomb in the White House, a mine in the Vatican, the death of Mao Ze-Tung, and [an] earthquake in Paris could not have echoed through the consciousness of every man in the world like the operation at Munich. The Olympiad arouses the people's interest and attention more than anything else in the world. The choice of the Olympics, from a purely propagandistic viewpoint, was 100 percent successful. It was like painting the name of Palestine on a mountain that can be seen from the four corners of the earth."

THE MUNICH MASSACRE

The PLO groups continued their war on Israel, attacking El Al airliners in Athens and Zurich and bombing the airline's offices. In 1970, they claimed responsibility for the fatal crash of a Swiss plane and later hijacked five airliners in three days. As a result, Britain, West Germany, and Switzerland agreed to release Palestinians from their prisons.

However, "bombing attacks on El Al offices do not serve our cause," argued Fuad al-Shamali of Black September, one of the PLO groups. "We have to kill their most important and most famous people. Since we cannot come close to their statesmen, we have to kill artists and sportsmen."

On the night of September 5, 1972, during the Munich Olympic Games, eight Black September terrorists burst into the dormitory of the Israeli athletes, killing two on the spot and taking nine others hostage. They demanded the release of 236 Palestinians held in Israeli jails and safe passage to any Arab country—except Jordan, where they had recently been outlawed, or Lebanon—and threatened to kill a hostage every two hours until their demands were met. After 15 hours of tense negotiation, the Germans agreed that the terrorists and their hostages would be taken by two helicopters to a nearby airbase so that they could board an airliner to

German police take up positions outside of the Israeli athletes' dormitory in the Olympic village at Munich in September 1972. Two athletes were killed in the attack by Black September terrorists, and nine others taken hostage. They, and five terrorists, later died in a firefight with the police.

30 INTERNATIONAL TERRORISM

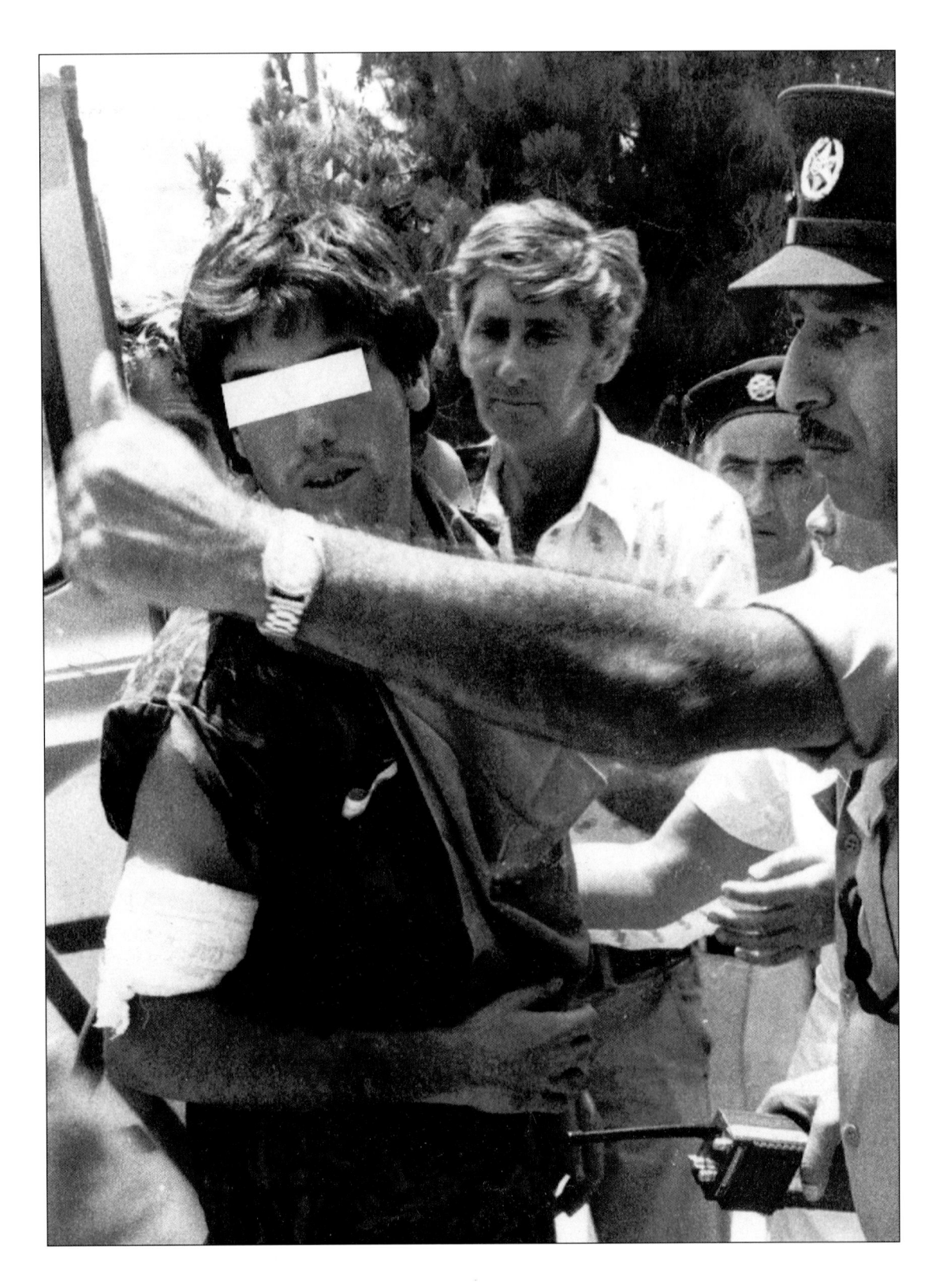

In June 1976, Palestinian terrorists hijacked an Air France airliner, forcing it to fly to Entebbe, Uganda. Six days later, a commando of Israeli paratroopers released all the hostages and killed the terrorists. Here, a wounded paratrooper is helped from an ambulance on return to Tel Aviv.

take them to Egypt, where the exchange of prisoners would take place. (However the Egyptians, for some reason, later withdrew their permission for the plane to land.)

A DISASTROUS FAILURE

When the helicopters landed at the airbase, four terrorists emerged. Two went to inspect the airliner, and two guarded the helicopters, while the other four remained inside with their hostages. The West German police, however, had set up an ambush. Their sharpshooters opened fire and killed three terrorists in the open. At this, those inside the helicopters returned the fire and, it is believed, began to kill the hostages.

Suddenly, around midnight, one of the terrorists jumped from a helicopter and threw a grenade into the cabin behind him, which exploded. The ensuing exchange of shots lasted a further hour and a half, resulting in the death of two more terrorists and a German policeman. Finally, the remaining three terrorists surrendered, at which point it was discovered that all nine of the hostages had been killed.

The operation—on both sides—can be considered a disastrous failure. Black September had certainly attracted worldwide attention—it was calculated that nearly 900 million people had seen the events live on television—but they lost much international sympathy and support for their cause. As for the West Germans, they realized how inadequate their response had been. They rapidly set up a specially trained antiterrorist detachment called GSG-9 (*Grenzschutzgruppe Neun*). Five years later, it was called into action and its newly developed skills were amply demonstrated in Mogadishu, Somalia, when it successfully rescued all 86 hostages from a hijacked Lufthansa flight.

In France, the *Gendarmerie Nationale* established a *Groupe d'Intervention* (GIGN) as a dedicated counterterrorism unit, and in Britain, the Special Air Services regiment (SAS) obtained permission to set up counterrevolutionary warfare units. At that time, the U.S. did not follow the European example, resulting in the disastrously bungled attempt to free 52 hostages captured in the U.S. embassy in Tehran in April 1980.

In spite of the negative publicity that followed the Munich tragedy, Black September claimed success. Not until that time had a terrorist attempt achieved worldwide media coverage. It was no coincidence that, two years later, Yasser Arafat was invited to address the United Nations General Assembly and, shortly afterward, the PLO was granted "special observer" status. By the end of the 1970s, the PLO had established diplomatic relations with no fewer than 86 countries. A further consequence was that the PLO became a model for other international terrorist movements. In the 10 years between 1968 and 1978, the number of such organizations rose from 11 to 55; and their number is presently estimated at 64, although some are currently inactive.

In June 1985, Hizballah terrorists hijacked a TWA aircraft. Gradually, all those passengers who were not U.S. citizens, were released, until only 39 American male hostages remained. President Reagan persuaded the Israeli government to release more than 700 Shi'a prisoners in exchange.

YASSER ARAFAT

Born Mohammed Arafat in 1929, the future president of the Palestinian Council was soon nicknamed Yasser, meaning "easy," by his family. After the Arab-Israeli war of 1948, he graduated in civil engineering at Cairo University, and in 1956, he founded al-Fatah, a small terrorist group devoted to the freedom of Palestine. It was not until 1967 that al-Fatah was recognized by the PLO, and 12 months later, Arafat became the PLO leader.

For 20 years, the PLO continued to launch violent attacks on Israel and, despite his recognition by the United Nations in 1974, Arafat was considered by many to be a ruthless terrorist. However, in 1988, he announced that the PLO was prepared to recognize that Israel was a sovereign state and give up violence for diplomacy. In 1993, secret talks took place in Norway and these resulted in the signing of the Oslo Peace Accord with Israeli Prime Minister Yitzhak Rabin. In 1994, Arafat was elected the first president of the Palestinian Council, charged with governing the West Bank and the Gaza Strip. He then returned to Palestine, having spent nearly 40 years in exile.

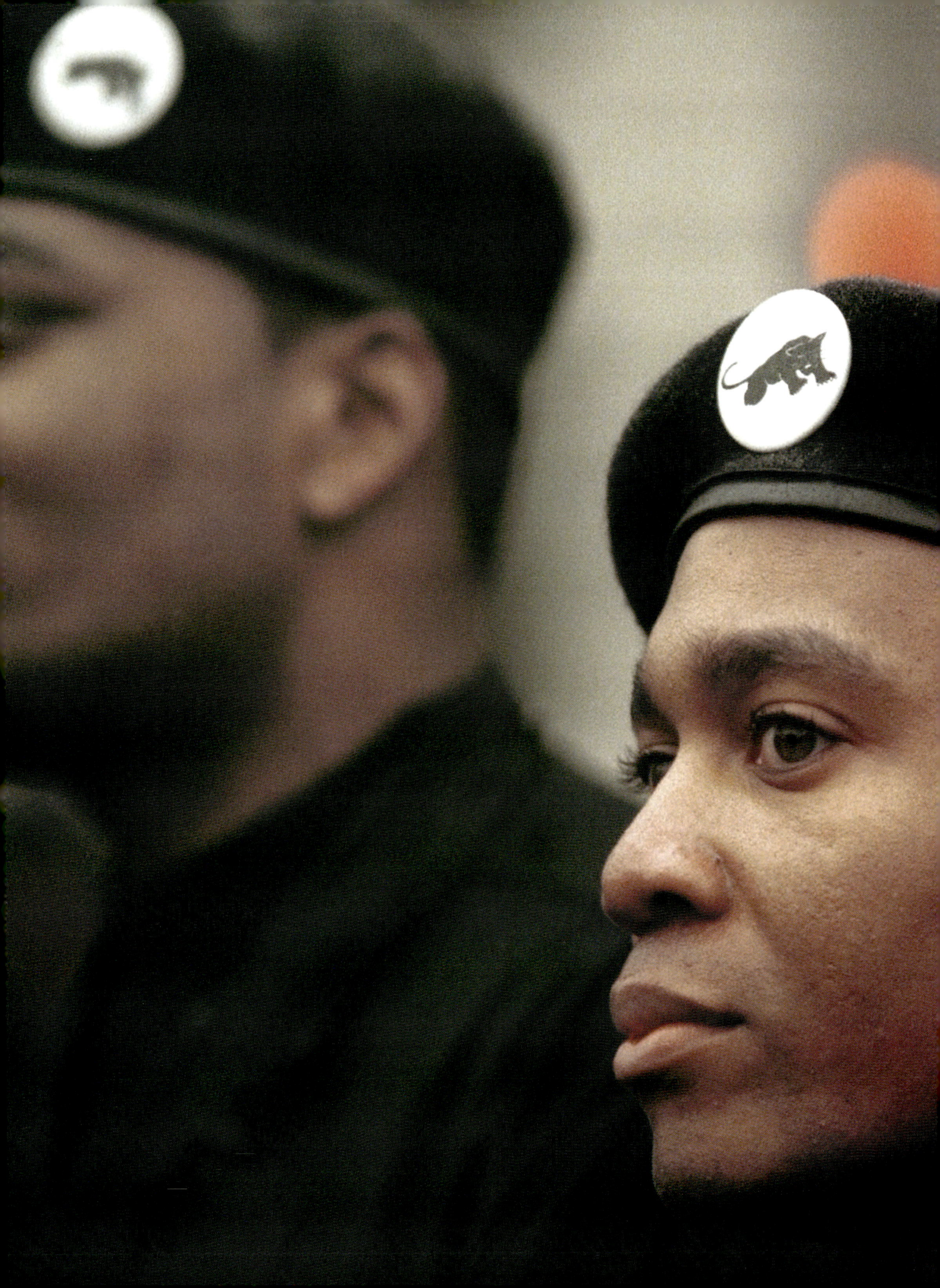

Urban Guerrillas

During the late 1960s and early 1970s, a new type of terrorist emerged, both in Europe and in the United States. These terrorists were not trying to secure some kind of national independence; they were not even making seriously concerted efforts to overthrow the oppression of their governments. This was a decade of protest: a vaguely expressed political opposition to the "established order" within their spheres of action. In fact, their violence afforded scarce possibility that they could effect any change in existing conditions, and it was little more than an outbreak of frustration at those conditions. Terrorists of this type preferred to describe themselves as "urban guerrillas"—although some had international connections of one kind or another.

THE RED BRIGADES

Among the more active, but in the end no more effective, were the Red Brigades (*Brigate Rosse*) of Italy. The founders of the Red Brigades were Renato Curcio and his wife, Margherita Cagol, a fellow student whom he married in 1970. Politically, they were so far to the left that they found common ground with members of the ultra-right. Curcio, in fact, had initially come to prominence as a member of an extreme-right organization, the New Order. It has even been alleged that the CIA secretly funded the Red Brigades when it became concerned about Communist influence within the Italian government.

Curcio and Cagol gathered a core of supporters from disillusioned university members, workers in industry, the Church, and Communists

Left: The Black Panther Party for Self-Defense was founded by Bobby Seale and Huey Newton in California in 1966. Members wore military-style uniforms, but did not indulge in unprovoked terrorist activities. In 1969, some members were killed in a lightning police raid in Chicago.

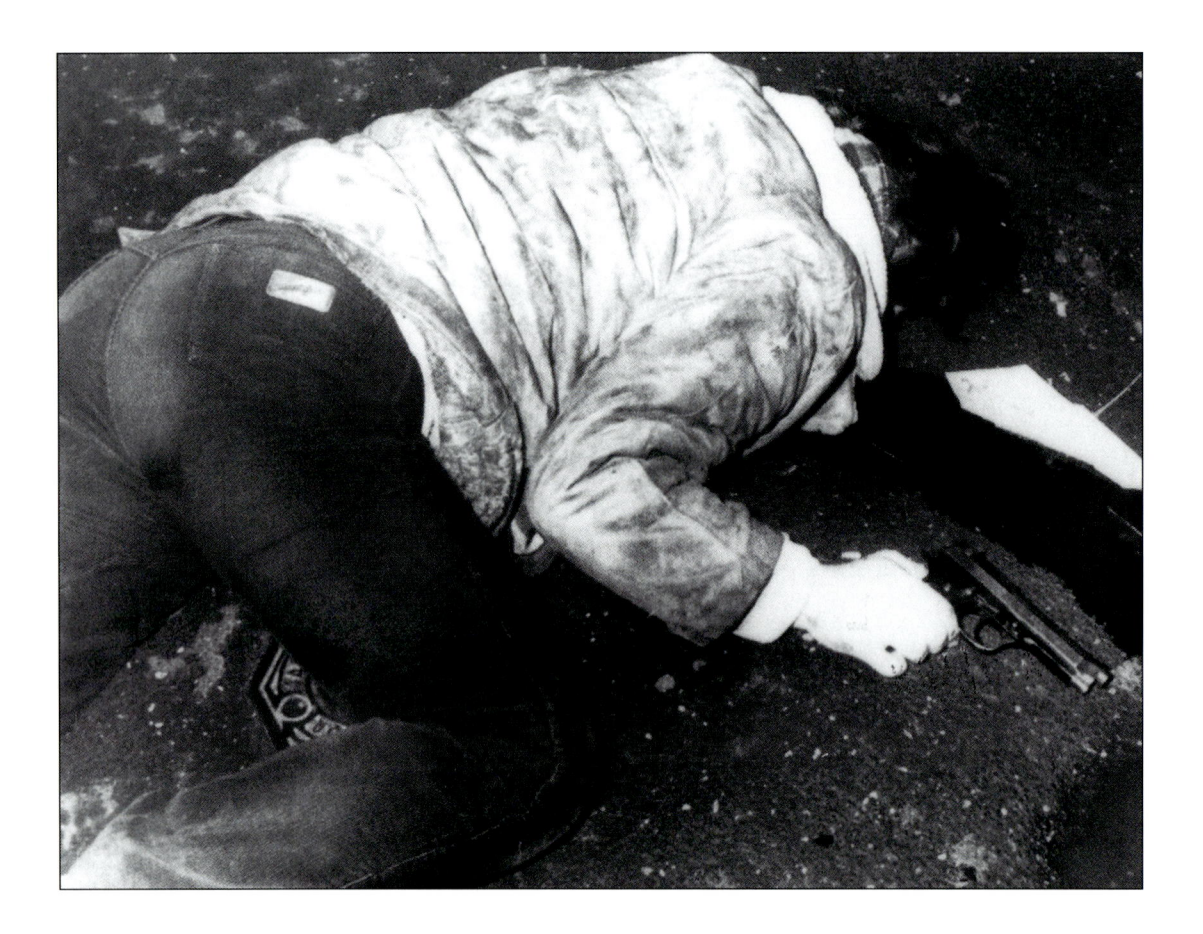

The body of Antonio Giustini lies in a pool of blood in the street. He was one of a group of terrorists from the Red Brigades who attacked an armored car outside a Rome supermarket in December 1984. Three others were seriously injured at the same time.

who had become dissatisfied with their party's policies. Early members of the Red Brigades were trained by exiles from Uruguay and Argentina who had taken **asylum** in Italy from their countries' ultra-military regimes.

Curcio's first action, in 1972, was to kidnap those he named "enemies of the people." These included a former personnel manager at the Fiat motor company and a trade union leader described as a "fascist." The victims were paraded in a mock trial before a "people's court," beaten up, and then released. And when some members of the Red Brigades were arrested, a state prosecutor was kidnapped in an effort to obtain their **acquittal**.

The early activities of the Red Brigades were centered around Milan. Later, operations were extended to other industrial centers, Turin and

Genoa, and kidnapping became a significant part of their activities—and an important source of funds. Editors and journalists were kidnapped to inhibit their exposing Red Brigades membership; teachers and university professors were targeted in an effort to ensure that the "correct" ideology was taught; and magistrates and jurors were attacked to subvert the passing of convictions in court. In 1973, John Paul Getty III, the grandson of the American financier, was kidnapped. His grandfather initially refused to pay a ransom of $3 million, and agreed only after receiving the young man's severed ear in the mail. Italian police did eventually find the victim, five months after his capture.

BRINGING CURCIO TO TRIAL

In 1974, police captured Curcio and imprisoned him. A few months later, his wife led an armed raid on the prison and released him. In 1975, he kidnapped a member of the Gancia wine and aperitif family, holding him in a "people's prison," a lonely farmhouse in Piedmont. When the *carabinieri* (Italian police) stormed the farmhouse, Margharita was shot and killed, but Curcio escaped, and was not captured for another year.

The trial of Curcio and other arrested members of the Red Brigades was delayed by more acts of terrorism. When it eventually opened in 1978, the head of one of the antiterrorist squads was shot dead, and a leading politician, Aldo Moro, was kidnapped on March 16. A former prime minister, Moro had played a crucial role in persuading the Christian Democrats to make a "historic compromise" with the Communists in return for their support of the Christian Democrat government in the fight against terrorism. Pleas for his release came from many prominent people, including Kurt Waldheim, secretary-general of the United Nations and the Pope himself ("I beg you on my knees," he pleaded). But on May 10, 1978, the bullet-ridden body of Aldo Moro was found in the trunk of a car in a street in Rome, just halfway between the headquarters of the Christian Democrats and the Communist Party.

> ## PATRICIO PEZI
>
> **Patricio Pezi, the leader of the Turin branch of the Red Brigades, stated their policy clearly and concisely, in words that echo those of Carlo Pisacane:**
>
> "First phase, armed propaganda…Second phase, that of armed support…Third phase, the civil war and victory. In essence, we were the embryo, the skeleton of the future…the ruling class of tomorrow in a Communist society….
>
> "The most pessimistic [people] thought that within 20 years the war would be won, some said within five, ten. All, however, thought that we were living through the most difficult moment, that gradually things would become easier."

Following the jailing of Curcio for life, the Red Brigades became more strongly organized. Their violence increased, and they established stronger links with other terrorist organizations. On December 17, 1981, they kidnapped U.S. Army Brigadier General James Dozier (the highest-ranking NATO officer in Italy) from his apartment in Verona. However, a month later, members of an elite Italian antiterrorist unit freed him in a lightning raid in Padua. In 1984, the Red Brigades claimed responsibility for the assassination of Leamon Hunt, the U.S. chief of the Sinai Multinational Force and Observer Group.

However, the Red Brigades were broken up when many members turned informer, and by 1985, the Italian government announced that 1,280 terrorists were in jail. French and Italian units captured many more during 1989, and the number of surviving members was estimated at less than 50, with most believed to be in hiding in countries outside Italy. Nevertheless, in March 2002, the Red Brigades resurfaced, claiming responsibility for the assassination of Italian politician Marco Biagi.

Leading Italian politician Aldo Moro, a former prime minister, was kidnapped by the Red Brigades in March 1978, as the trial of several terrorists opened. This photograph of Moro was issued by his captors, but, despite pleas for his release, his bullet-ridden body was found two months later.

40   INTERNATIONAL TERRORISM

Andreas Baader, who—with his girlfriend Gudrun Ensslin and leftist journalist Ulrike Meinhof—founded the Red Army Faction in Germany in 1970. He was captured after a firefight at his bomb-making factory in 1972. He was found dead in his prison cell—reportedly a suicide—in 1977.

THE RED ARMY FACTION

Contemporary with the Red Brigades, but distinctly different in origin, was the Red Army Faction (RAF; popularly known as the Baader-Meinhof gang) and its related organization, the Second of June Movement—named for the anniversary of the killing of student Benno Ohnsberg during a demonstration in 1967. They came from the "alternative" background of **communes** and dropout student groups—mostly the children of rich parents—in late-1960s West Germany, and their "revolutionary" terrorism was combined with sexual freedom and the use of drugs. Wrote Michael "Bommi" Baumann, a leading Second of June member:

"With me it all began with rock music and long hair…it was like this: if you had long hair, things were suddenly like they are for the blacks. They threw us out of joints, they cursed at us and ran after us—all you had was trouble. So you start building contacts with a few people like yourself."

They harbored contempt for the bourgeois (middle-class) values of their

The German counterterrorist unit GSG9 had a brilliant success in rescuing passengers and crew from a Lufthansa aircraft hijacked to Mogadishu, Somalia, in October 1977. Here, the German Chancellor, Helmut Schmidt, congratulates the commander of the unit on its return.

fellow Germans. "All they can think about is some hairspray, a vacation in Spain, and a tiled bathroom," said newspaper columnist Ulricke Meinhof.

In their announcements, the RAF compared themselves to the Black Panthers, the African-American radical group active in the 1960s, and quoted one of its leaders, Eldridge Cleaver. "The RAF are putting the words of Cleaver," they said, "into practice."

In spite of its anti-establishment background, there was nevertheless a political dimension to West German terrorism, centered on opposition to the war in Vietnam. "To my mind, it wasn't just an international question," terrorist Hans Joachim Klein explained, "but also an internal problem. The B52s stopped over at Wiesbaden on their way from Vietnam."

AN INTERNATIONAL TERRORIST OPERATION

The RAF, who had begun by carrying out armed raids on banks and setting bombs in cities, mounted their first international terrorist operation following the United States Air Forces' mining of Haiphong Harbor in North Vietnam in May 1972. In a bomb attack on the Fifth Army Corp's officers' mess in Frankfurt, one person was killed and 13 injured.

The following month, the German police received an anonymous tip-off and staked out a garage where the RAF was building bombs. When Baader and two associates arrived, there was a fierce firefight, which ceased only when Baader ran out of ammunition. Altogether, five leading members of the gang were rounded up and put on trial in a special courtroom built in Stammheim Jail. Many attempts were made to obtain their release: the West German embassy in Stockholm was seized; three separate plane hijackings were organized by the PLO in support; and a leading German industrialist was kidnapped and murdered. However, the German government considered the Baader-Meinhof gang too dangerous to yield to these demands, and all five were sentenced to long terms of imprisonment. In 1976, Ulricke Meinhof was found dead in her cell and Baader died, in similar circumstances, the following year.

Following the failure of the Mogadishu hijacking, Andreas Baader was found dead in his prison cell; it was announced as suicide, although some people still maintain he was murdered. At his burial, masked sympathizers held this banner commemorating his death and that of Gudrun Ensslin and fellow-terrorist Jan-Carl Raspe.

It was not the end of the RAF, however. Before the reunification of Germany in 1990, East Germany provided support and training for a continuing campaign in West Germany. In 1993, the RAF was credited with the bombing of a new prison, and during the Gulf War, they attacked the U.S. embassy in Bonn. However, current estimates put the active membership at only 10 to 20.

OTHER EUROPEAN ORGANIZATIONS

In France, after the student and labor unrest of May 1968, workers began to demonstrate against the continuing rule of President Charles de Gaulle.

> ## THE BIRTH OF THE RAF
>
> Andreas Baader was a petty criminal drawn to the student protest movement by the excitement it offered. In 1968, he and his girlfriend Gudrun Ensslin firebombed two Frankfurt department stores, allegedly in protest against the Vietnam War. They were jailed, but later released on parole, pending appeal, and they then went on the run.
>
> Ulrike Meinhof was a well-known leftist journalist who defended the actions of Baader and Ensslin in her columns. Baader was recaptured in 1970, but was allowed to visit a Berlin library under guard. There, Meinhof, Ensslin, and two others, all armed, engineered his escape through a window. The Red Army Faction was born and named in imitation of the Japanese Red Army terrorists. Members then traveled to Amman in Jordan to receive guerrilla training from the PLO.

A movement calling itself the Proletarian Left organized an illegal armed group, the New Popular Resistance, but this soon broke up, and in 1974, a new organization was formed, the *Groupes d'Action Révolutionnaire Internationale* (GARI). The GARI saw itself as truly international, proclaiming "the fight, by direct action, against the Francoist dictatorship, against capitalism, against the state, for the liberation of Spain, Europe, and the world." They kidnapped the head of the Bank of Bilbao in Paris and carried out 25 assassinations and five hold-ups in France and Belgium.

The GARI were soon superseded by the *Brigades Internationales* (BI), reportedly inspired by the teachings of Chinese Communist leader Mao Ze-dong. For three years, the BI carried out a series of assassinations against foreign diplomats. However, bitter disagreements broke out, and the BI soon gave way to the NAPAP (Armed Groups for Popular Self-

Government), who concentrated their attacks upon large automobile works; and then, in 1978, roused by the deaths of Ulricke Meinhof and Andreas Baader, came the most famous of French urban guerrilla groups, Direct Action (*Action Directe*).

For 10 years, Direct Action mounted attacks on industrial establishments, police stations, government offices, radio and television stations, town halls, and banks—mostly French institutions, but including the Chase Manhattan bank. They maintained contact with Belgian groups, and in 1985, they announced their collaboration with the RAF. On August 8, 1985, a joint DA-RAF "commando" (named "George Jackson" after a Black Panther who had been murdered in prison in 1970) attacked the U.S. Air Force base in Frankfurt, killing three servicemen.

The group's activities continued through 1986 and included an invasion of the offices of Interpol; and in September of that year, the French government passed special counterterrorist laws. By now, many members of Direct Action were in prison and, with the arrest of their leaders in 1987, urban guerrilla activity in France declined. In the island of Corsica, however, the Corsican National Liberation Front, which emerged in 1976, has continued a campaign of terrorism against French authorities.

CARLOS THE JACKAL

One of the most elusive and violent of international terrorists was born in Venezuela in 1949. Christened Ilich Ramirez Sanchez, he became known as Carlos "the Jackal." He was rumored to be the "mastermind" behind the Black September attack on Israeli athletes at the 1972 Olympics. He gained further notoriety in 1975, when he led a combined team of German and Palestinian terrorists who took 70 hostages at a Vienna meeting of ministers from the Organization of Petroleum Exporting Countries (OPEC).

Carlos also organized attacks for the Japanese Red Army, including the occupation of the French embassy in the Netherlands in 1974 and the bombing of a Paris discotheque in which two people were killed and

46 INTERNATIONAL TERRORISM

Ilich Ramirez Sanchez, known as "Carlos the Jackal," appears in court in Paris in November 2000. His trial coincided with that of his German accomplice, Hans-Joachim Klein, in Frankfurt. Both were jailed for the 1975 kidnapping of OPEC ministers in Vienna, in which three people died.

35 injured. He was also believed to be responsible for the attempt on the life of Edward Sieff, the president of Marks & Spencer, in London. In all, he claimed to have killed 83 people.

Warrants for Carlos' arrest were issued in five European countries, but he continued his activities into the 1980s. In 1991, he was ordered to leave his hideout in Syria, and was turned away by Iraq and Libya. He found refuge in Sudan in 1993, but was captured there in August 1994 and carried off by French agents. He stood trial in France for the murder in 1975 of two agents of the French DST and a Lebanese, and, after 20 years of terrorism, was sentenced to life imprisonment. He left the court raising his clenched fist in the air and exclaiming, *"Vive la revolution!"*

THE BLACK PANTHERS AND THE WEATHERMEN

The Black Panther Party for Self-Defense was founded in California in 1966, following Stokely Carmichael's impassioned speech at a rally in Greenwood, Mississippi: "We have been saying 'Freedom' for six years," he cried. "What we are going to start saying now is 'Black Power.' " However, the Black Panthers, although they appeared in public in military-style uniforms—and sometimes carrying rifles—were largely defensive, and did not indulge in unprovoked terrorist attacks. Nevertheless, they became an example for the West German RAF, as well as for the Weathermen and related terrorist groups in the United States.

The Weathermen were first heard of at a convention of the Students for a Democratic Society (SDS) in Chicago, in June 1969. They distributed a **manifesto** there, headed with a line from a Bob Dylan song: "You don't need a weatherman to know which way the wind blows."

The Weathermen, who sprang from an SDS chapter at New York's Columbia University, advocated urban violence in the U.S. as a protest against the war in Vietnam. Shortly before midnight on October 6, as the prelude to what they announced as their "Days of Rage," helmeted Weathermen blew up a memorial to Chicago policemen in the city's

Haymarket Square. In the days that followed, they wrecked cars and smashed windows in the business district. More than 300 people were arrested. A police official declared, "We now feel that it is kill or be killed."

Subsequently, the Weathermen concentrated, together with another underground group known as Revolutionary Force 9, on a series of bombings of business property. They caused enormous damage, and nearly 50 deaths resulted, but most of these were of Weathermen, who blew themselves up in the course of manufacturing bombs. In March 1970, for example, three were killed in a bomb factory they had established in the Manhattan townhouse belonging to the parents of one of two survivors of the explosion. He escaped and formed the Weather Underground, which continued to commit robberies and bombings through the 1970s.

The Chicago police memorial has since been rebuilt. However, now it is inside police headquarters and unreachable, "except maybe by helicopter or from the sewers," a commentator has recently remarked.

Members of the Black Panther party sometimes carried arms, but their principal concern was with self-defense. Nevertheless, their example was cited by the Red Army Faction, who claimed to be putting their principles into practice.

THE JAPANESE RED ARMY

Formed around 1970 by Fusako Shigenobu, the Japanese Red Army (JRA) is a tiny terrorist organization devoted to "world revolution." During the 1970s, they carried out a series of international attacks, including the massacre of 26 people in 1972 at Lod Airport in Israel, the hijacking of two Japanese airliners, and the attempted takeover of the U.S. embassy in Kuala Lumpur, Malaysia. In April 1988, the JRA was believed to be responsible for the bombing of a U.S. officers' club in Naples, Italy, in which five people were killed. At the same time, a JRA member was arrested while carrying explosives on the New Jersey Turnpike and jailed. In 1996, another member was jailed in the United States, and Fusako Shigenobu herself was arrested in Japan in 2000. Since her arrest, the JRA has formed cells in Asian cities such as Manila and Singapore.

THE SYMBIONESE LIBERATION ARMY

The smallest, and the strangest, of American terrorist groups called itself the Symbionese Liberation Army (SLA)—"symbionese" apparently meaning "living together." The SLA was the brainchild of Donald DeFreeze (known as "Cinque"), who escaped from prison in March 1973. He holed up in the San Francisco Bay area with Mizmoon Soltysik, and together they began to write plans for a "Symbionese Nation." Later, they were joined by a handful of "revolutionaries," and began to steal guns and rent hideouts.

In November 1973, the group decided that their first action would be the assassination of Dr. Marcus Foster, a schools superintendent from Oakland whom they accused of being a "fascist." However, the choice of a prominent local black leader was a fatal error, and lost them any public sympathy. Two men, Joe Remiro and Russ Little, were arrested for Foster's

> ## THE BRITISH UNDERGROUND
>
> **In Britain, a few students and members of the "underground," calling themselves the Angry Brigade, attempted to imitate the RAF. They set off several bombs—notably outside the house of the Home Secretary in 1971—but in December 1972, four members were found guilty of "conspiracy to cause explosions," after a record 111-day trial, and the Angry Brigade sank without trace.**

murder in January 1974. Little was subsequently acquitted on retrial, but Remiro was committed to prison for life.

Shortly after, the SLA carried out their next action: the kidnapping of Patricia Hearst, the 19-year-old granddaughter heiress of the newspaper mogul, William Hearst, on February 4. The kidnappers demanded Patricia's parents provide $70-worth of food to each poor person in California, which, by their calculation, made a total of $400 million. The Hearsts offered $2 million in advance and a further $4 million if Patricia was released unharmed. Some food was distributed in a program named "People in Need," but the SLA responded with a tape-recorded message from Patricia along with a photo of her carrying a submachine gun in front of the SLA's symbol, a seven-headed cobra. On the tape, she announced that she had taken the name "Tania" and that she had decided to remain with the SLA "and fight."

On April 15, five members of the SLA, including "Tania," were captured on video robbing a bank in San Francisco. On May 16, she covered the escape of two shoplifting comrades in Los Angeles, firing shots into the air. The next day, investigators discovered an SLA hideout in Los Angeles: 400 police and FBI agents shot it out with the six occupants before the house burned down, but "Tania" was not among them.

The SLA was effectively finished, but its remaining members were not captured until September 1975. At Patricia's trial, famous criminal lawyer F. Lee Bailey argued that she had been **brainwashed**—blindfolded, locked in a closet, humiliated, and starved. Nevertheless, she was found guilty and sentenced to seven years in jail in March 1976. President Carter commuted the sentence in February 1979, and on January 20, 2001, among his outgoing gestures, President Clinton granted Patricia a full pardon.

Patricia Hearst, who named herself "Tania" when she sided with the Symbionese Liberation Army, is escorted into a San Francisco courtroom in 1976. Found guilty of armed involvement in a bank robbery, she was sentenced to seven years in jail.

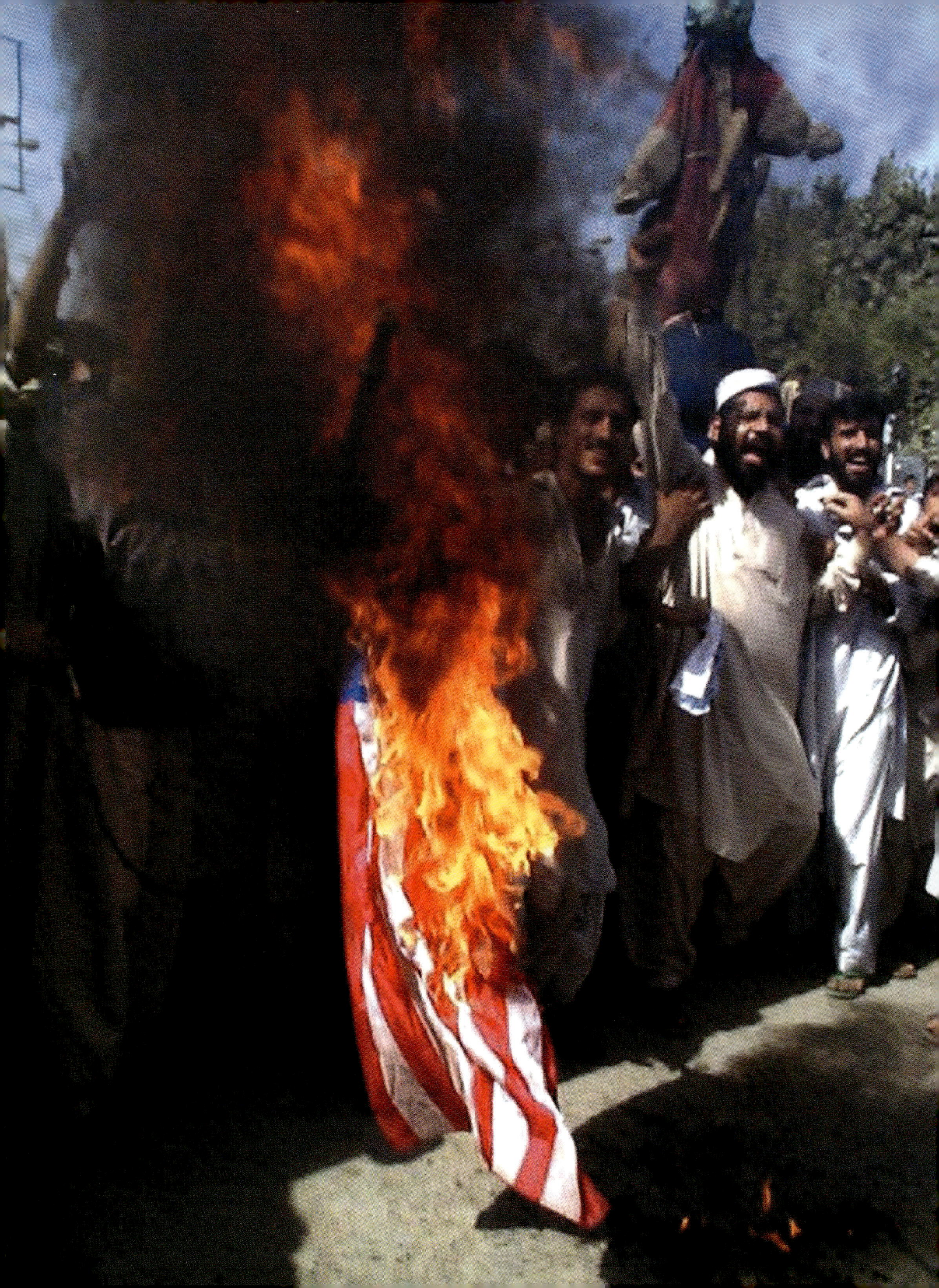

Terrorism and Religion

So far, all the terrorist movements described have been political—or largely so. The actions of the principal organizations were directed either against their own governments or in an effort to obtain standing as a separate national state. As for the smaller protest groups, they were avowedly political, and mostly of a leftward-leaning persuasion.

For the past quarter-century, however, the activities of many "ethno-nationalist" movements have declined and instead, a wide range of terrorist groups have come into being, whose motivation is overridingly religious. Although the revolution against the Shah in Iran in 1979 was the inspiration for many Islamic terrorists, this rise in religious terrorism is not confined to the Muslim world. Indeed, since the 1980s, it is found among major elements of all the world's religions, as well as smaller sects.

"I ACTED ON ORDERS FROM GOD"

"I have no regrets," said Yigal Amir, the young Jew who assassinated Prime Minister Yitzhak Rabin of Israel in 1995. "I acted alone and on orders from God." It is words like these that we have heard from so many extremists in recent years—Muslims, Hindus, Japanese, Jews, and Christians.

Not that the connection between religion and terrorism is a modern phenomenon. The word "zealot," for example, comes from a Jewish sect that was active in Palestine in 66–73 B.C. The Zealots carried out ruthless assassinations, not only against the occupying Romans, but also against other Jews who were considered insufficiently orthodox in their religion.

Left: Just one week after the destruction of the World Trade Center on September 11, 2001, demonstrators claiming to support Osama bin Laden set fire to the Stars and Stripes in Karachi, Pakistan, and chant anti-U.S. and pro-Al Qaeda slogans.

The word "assassin" itself is derived from the *Hashishim*, a branch of the Islamic **Shi'a** sect that was active between 1090 and 1272. Their name means "hashish-eaters"; new recruits were given the drug hashish and shown—either in a vision or, perhaps, in reality—a beautiful garden, which, they were told, was the heaven they would immediately attain should they be killed while carrying out their attacks. This attitude toward **martyrdom** has colored Islamic terrorism ever since. There was also a political dimension to the assassins—as well as Christian crusaders, their targets included Islamic leaders who were judged unworthy—but they believed their actions to be a divine duty.

In an identical way, the word "thug" comes from *Thuggee*, a Hindu religious cult that terrorized India from the 7th through the 19th centuries. They waylaid and ritually strangled unwary travelers on special holy days as sacrificial offerings to the goddess of terror, Kali.

MODERN ISLAMIC TERRORISM

"The world as it is today is how others [have] shaped it," wrote the Ayatollah Baqer al-Sadr. "We have two choices, either to accept it with submission, which means letting Islam die, or to destroy it, so that we can construct the world as Islam requires." The Ayatollahs are the leaders of the Shi'a sect, which has been the principal exponent of violent opposition to what they regard as attacks on their fundamental religion. In Lebanon, the Shi'a terrorist organization Hizballah ("Party of God") stated in 1985: "We, the sons of Hizballah, consider ourselves a part of the world Islamic community, attacked at once by the tyrants and the arrogance of the East and the West… Our way is one of radical combat against depravity, and America is the original root of depravity."

In protest against Israel's invasion of Lebanon in 1982, Hizballah's spiritual leader, Ayatollah Muhammad Hussein Fadlallah, wrote:

"This invasion was confronted by the Islamic factor, which had its roots in the Islamic Revolution in Iran. And, throughout these affairs, America

TERRORISM AND RELIGION 55

In October 1997, agents of the Israeli intelligence service, Mossad, attempted to assassinate a leading member of the Palestinian terrorist organization, Hamas. The attempt provoked widespread indignation, and Israel was forced to free Sheikh Yassin, Hamas' founder—seen here attending a rally in Gaza City after his release.

was the common denominator. America was generally perceived as the great nemesis behind the problems of the region, due to its support for Israel and many local reactionary regimes, and because it distanced itself from all causes of liberty and freedom in the area."

IRANIAN REVOLUTION

Iran, once known as Persia, is the heartland of the Shi'a branch of Islamic belief. The Shah ruled Iran until 1979, but protests against his Westernizing policies began in the 1960s and led to the exile of Ayatollah Ruhollah

FUNDAMENTALISM

Before the 1980s, the word "fundamentalism" had a specific meaning in North America. It referred to organized evangelical Christian religious groups who adhered strictly to the Bible.

Islamic fundamentalists adhere to what they consider the basic tenets of the Koran, the laws dictated by the prophet Muhammad in the seventh century. Modernist Muslims—probably the majority of Islam—accept most Western scientific and political ideas. A conservative minority, however, inspired by the "mullahs," believes in a strict interpretation of the Koran. Most followers of this belief are impoverished, uneducated young men who have grown up in refugee camps. Inspired by the teachings of the mullahs in the mosques, specific verses from the Koran are used as justification for a violent defense of Islamic tradition, particularly against Jews and Americans.

Basically, Islam is a religion opposed to violence. The taking of innocent life—even in war—is strictly forbidden. Suicide, too, is condemned in Muhammad's laws: those who commit it are consigned to the fires of Hell. Islamic fundamentalists, however, cite passages in the Koran that promise paradise to those who die in jihad—"struggling in the way of Allah." This is the interpretation of present-day terrorists.

Khomeini in 1964. He spent some years in Iraq, but then settled near Paris, France, where he called for the overthrow of the Shah. Serious rioting broke out in Iran in 1978, and when the Shah and his family fled in January 1979, Khomeini returned to the country and was at once hailed as its leader. He declared Iran a republic in March 1979.

On November 4, 1979, Khomeini's followers, alleging American involvement in plans to restore the Shah, stormed the U.S. embassy in Tehran and took 66 people hostage. President Carter's efforts to secure their release failed, as did a U.S. Army commando attempt to rescue them by helicopters in April 1980. It was not until January 20, 1981, that intervention by Algeria obtained their freedom.

The crisis seriously weakened President Carter's bid for a second term, and Ronald Reagan was elected president in November 1980. However, Reagan's second term was marked by the "Irangate" scandal in 1986. It was revealed that, despite tough antiterrorist talk in public, the administration had started secret negotiations to sell arms to Iran and channel the profits illegally to the Contra guerrillas in Nicaragua.

At this time, Iran was engaged in a bitter war with Iraq arising from a border dispute. The conflict lasted from 1980 through 1988, with heavy loss of life, and, after early successes, the Iranian army began to suffer

More than 300 miles (483 km) from the Iranian capital of Tehran, the charred remains of a U.S. Army helicopter lie beside a second, undamaged one in the Dasht-e-Kavir Desert. The attempt to rescue 66 U.S. embassy employees held hostage in Tehran failed, with the loss of eight lives.

58 INTERNATIONAL TERRORISM

serious shortages of equipment while the West was supplying Iraq openly. The United Nations eventually obtained a cease-fire in July 1988.

The rise of Islamic fundamentalism, therefore, can be traced directly to the success of the revolution in Iran. Ayatollah Khomeini imposed strict Islamic law according to the Koran and successfully weathered the U.S. embassy hostage crisis and the drawn-out war with Iraq. Before his death in 1989, he further damaged relations with the West by pronouncing a *fatwa*

Hizballah (the Army of God) is dedicated to the establishment of an Islamic state in Lebanon, where it has been responsible for many anti-U.S. attacks. Here—equipped with military camouflage fatigues, and armed with a mortar and grenade launchers—members pose for the camera.

(death sentence) on Salman Rushdie, British author of the novel *The Satanic Verses*, which he condemned as "blasphemous."

Under his successor, Hashemi Rafshanjani, Iran began to improve relations with the West, but these deteriorated during the Gulf War of 1991 and the subsequent signing of the Israeli–PLO peace accord in 1993. The breakup of the Soviet Union in 1991 led to Iran strengthening links with the newly independent Islamic states of Central Asia; and in 1995, the United States announced total trade and investment **sanctions** against the country in an attempt to restrict its involvement in international terrorism.

ISLAMIC TERRORIST GROUPS

"We must strive to export our Revolution throughout the world," declared Khomeini, "and must abandon any idea of not doing so, for Islam is the champion of all oppressed people." And so, with Iranian encouragement and support, an increasing number of terrorist groups began to emerge.

In Lebanon, the Hizballah (Army of God) established itself in the suburbs of Beirut and the southern part of the country, and it has since set up cells in every part of the world. It receives substantial aid, both financial and in arms supplies, together with training, from Iran and neighboring Syria. Apart from its political aim to establish power in Lebanon, Hizballah is violently opposed to the state of Israel and to any attempt by the West to secure peace in the Middle East. It has been involved in many anti-U.S. attacks, including the suicide truck-bombing of both the U.S. embassy and the Marine barracks in Beirut in October 1983 and of the embassy annex in September 1984.

Based in Egypt, Islamic Jihad emerged in the late 1970s. Aiming to overthrow the moderate Egyptian government and establish an Islamic state, this group assassinated Egyptian president Anwar Sadat in 1981. It also attacked U.S. and Israeli interests in Egypt and abroad using car bombs. Islamic Jihad has built up a network outside Egypt, which includes Yemen, Afghanistan, Pakistan, Sudan, Lebanon, and Britain.

A conference to discuss peace between Israel and the Arab states provoked many demonstrations of protest in the Arab world. Here, Shi'ite supporters of Hizballah march in Beirut, Lebanon, in October 1991, proclaiming "Death to America, Death to Israel."

Another Egyptian terrorist organization is the Islamic Group (Al-Gama'a al-Islamiya), which at one time had a hard-core membership of several thousand, together with as many sympathizers. It claimed responsibility for the June 1995 assassination attempt on Egyptian president Hosni Mubarak in Addis Ababa, Ethiopia. Following Al-Gama'a attacks on tourists in 1997, the Egyptian government initiated a crackdown, and there has consequently been a decrease in its strength. The group who bombed the World Trade Center in New York City in February 1993 had obtained a *fatwa* from the Al-Gama'a spiritual leader Sheikh Omar Abd al-Rahman, who is currently imprisoned in the U.S.

THE ABU NIDAL ORGANIZATION AND HAMAS

The Abu Nidal Organization is derived from Black September, which split from the PLO in 1974. It is led by Sabri al-Banna, but gets its name from

TERRORISM AND RELIGION   61

its financial controller, Abu Nidal—in 1988, he was said to have available funds of some $400 million, including the profits of a multinational arms company in Poland. Originally based in Palestine, the ANO relocated to Iraq in 1989, but maintains a presence in refugee camps in Lebanon. It is a **mercenary** terrorist organization, and has been employed as a "hired gun" by Syria, Iraq, and Libya—although its operations in the latter country, and also in Egypt, were closed down in 1999. It has carried out terrorist attacks in 20 countries, killing or injuring nearly 900 people.

The Palestine Liberation Front (PLF) is another breakaway group, dating from the mid-1970s. It was originally based in Tunisia, from where a team of four carried out the seizure of the Italian cruise liner, *Achille*

Palestinian suicide bombers have carried out sporadic attacks on the civilian population of Israel for many years. Here, Israeli investigators examine the devastation at a site in Tel Aviv, where a suicide bomber killed more than 20 people in March 1996.

Lauro. They attempted to ransom the vacationers on board for 50 Palestinian terrorists in Israeli prisons and murdered an American tourist, Leon Klinghofer, who was confined in a wheelchair, dumping his body in the sea. Eventually, Yasser Arafat negotiated a deal, promising the hijackers a safe return to Tunisia after they had landed the ship's passengers in Alexandria, Egypt. However, U.S. Navy fighter planes intercepted the EgyptAir plane carrying the four and forced it to land in Sicily, where Italian police arrested the terrorists. The U.S. State Department announced a $250,000 reward for the capture of the PLF leader, Abu Abbas, but he remains at liberty, and the organization is now based in Iraq.

In Palestine, the largest terrorist movement is Hamas, which counts thousands of members and sympathizers. It emerged in 1987, and its aim is to establish an Islamic state in place of Israel. Funded in part by Iran, it also receives support from private benefactors in other Arab countries and from fundraising efforts in Western Europe and North America. It has not specifically attacked non-Israeli targets; however, in 1999, it was banned from the kingdom of Jordan.

Other Palestinian organizations are the Democratic Front for the Liberation of Palestine and the Palestine Islamic Jihad (PIJ). In July 2000, the PIJ threatened to attack U.S. interests if the embassy was moved from Tel Aviv to Jerusalem.

ISLAMIC TERRORISM WORLDWIDE

Pakistan harbors at least four Islamic terrorist groups, active since 1990, whose primary aim is the liberation of Kashmir from India and its unification with Pakistan. Harakat ul-Ansar (HUA), which counts several thousand armed supporters, was responsible for the kidnapping of U.S. nationals in New Delhi in 1994 in an attempt to secure the release of their leader, Maulana Masood Azhar. Upon his release in a hostage exchange in 1999, Azhar formed the Army of Mohammed, which was suspected of the terrorist attack on the Indian parliament in December 2001. The HUA has

THE KILLING OF DANIEL PEARL

The National Movement for the Restoration of Pakistani Sovereignty, a group previously unknown in Pakistan, claimed responsibility for the kidnapping and subsequent murder of *Wall Street Journal* reporter Daniel Pearl in January 2002. The organization sent e-mails announcing his kidnapping, and a videotape received by U.S. diplomats on February 21, 2002, confirmed that Pearl had been killed. FBI agents traced the e-mails to Fahad Naseem, who named British subject Ahmed Omar Saeed Sheikh as the instigator of the kidnapping. However, he was, presumably, not responsible for Pearl's death, because he was arrested on February 5, 2002.

Sheikh, who was educated at an English public school and was subsequently a student at the London School of Economics, had long been associated with Islamic extremists. He was arrested in India in 1994 and spent five years in jail before being released, with two others, in exchange for the passengers and crew of an Indian Airlines plane that had been hijacked to Kandahar, Afghanistan. Rumors have widely reported the involvement of the Pakistan intelligence service, ISI—many of whose members were supportive of the Taliban regime in Afghanistan—with Pakistan terrorist organizations.

diversified into the Harakat ul-Mujahidin, whose leader signed a *fatwa* in 1998 calling for attacks on U.S. and Western interests. The fourth group is Lashkar-e-Tayyiba, which is allied to a religious movement opposed to the work of American missionaries and has contacts with similar groups around the world, including the Philippines. All four organizations have been active, not only in Pakistan and Kashmir, but also in Afghanistan.

In the Philippines, the smallest (but the most radical and probably the best internationally connected) of the Islamic terrorist organizations is the Abu Sayyaf Group. It split from the Moro National Liberation Front in 1991, and its aim is to establish an independent state in western Mindanao and the Sulu Archipelago. In 2000, the group kidnapped 30 foreign nationals. A nonreligious Communist hit squad is the Alex Boncayao Brigade, which is believed to have been responsible for the 1989 murder of U.S. Army Colonel James Rowe.

An obscure, but dangerous, Islamic terrorist movement is Jamaat ul-Fuqra, which was responsible for a series of assassinations and firebombings across the United States in the 1980s. A number of members have been convicted of criminal violations, including murder and fraud, and others have set up isolated rural communes in North America, where they practice their faith, far removed from Western culture.

Finally, there is Al Qaeda, established by Osama bin Laden in the late 1980s, which is the subject of the following chapter.

TERRORISTS OF OTHER FAITHS

There is a fundamentalist Jewish terrorist organization within Israel. This is known as Kahane Chai ("Kahane Lives"), named after Meir Kahane, who founded both the Jewish Defense League and Kach ("Thus"), and who was assassinated by an Egyptian gunman in New York in 1990.

Kahane was born in New York City in 1932 and founded the Jewish Defense League in 1968. He emigrated to Israel with his family in 1971 and established Kach as a political party shortly thereafter. He ran unsuccessfully in two elections for the Knesset, the Israeli parliament, and in 1980, because of the violence of his anti-Arab speeches, was jailed. In 1984, he gained a seat in the Knesset, but, before the 1988 election, he was banned from running. That year, in a speech to university students in Los Angeles, he described the Arabs as "dogs" who "multiply like fleas" and who must either be expelled from Israel or eliminated.

LIBYA

The role of Libya in international terrorism has been an ambivalent one. While there appears to be no specifically Libyan terrorist organization, there is no doubt that Muammar al-Qaddafi's regime has in the past given sanctuary, training, and material support to many terrorist organizations and had also employed mercenary groups in state-sponsored attacks.

The German court has judged Libya's intelligence service responsible for the bombing of a Berlin disco in April 1986, which resulted in the deaths of two American servicemen. As a result, the U.S. Air Force launched air attacks against the Libyan capital, Tripoli. In retaliation, Libya hired the Japanese Red Army to attack U.S. diplomatic facilities in Jakarta, Indonesia, Madrid, and Rome over the following 12 months.

In December 1988, PanAm Flight 103 was blown out of the sky above Lockerbie, Scotland, with the loss of 270 lives, mostly American, and Libya was held responsible. In 1999, Qaddafi turned over two Libyans suspected of the atrocity, one of whom was found guilty before a Scottish court held in the Netherlands. Since that time, the Libyan leader has begun to make overtures to reestablish relations with the U.S., condemning the attacks of September 11, 2001, on New York and Washington, D.C., and taking action against his country's Muslim militants.

After his death, his son Binyamin renamed the organization Kahane Chai and was also jailed several times for his activities. The movement plotted to destroy Jerusalem's Dome of the Rock on Temple Mount, and claimed responsibility for several attacks on Palestinians in 1993; and in 1994, Baruch Goldstein, a Kach member, murdered 29 Palestinians praying in the al-Ibrahimi mosque, resulting in the Israeli government outlawing the organization. Following this, in 1995, Israel's prime minister, Yitzhak Rabin, was assassinated by a Kahane Chai supporter. On December 31, 2000, Binyamin Kahane and his wife Talia were shot dead by a Palestinian group calling themselves the Martyrs of the al-Aqsa Intifada.

NERVE GAS TERRORISM

The Japanese religious sect Aum Shinrikyo is infamous for its attack with sarin, a nerve gas, in the Tokyo subway on March 20, 1995, in which 12 people died and thousands were incapacitated.

The sect was founded in 1987 by 22-year-old Chizuo Matsumoto, who changed his name at that time to Asahara Shoko. Aum is Sanskrit for "the powers of creation and destruction in the universe," and Shinrikyo is "the teaching of the supreme truth." In August 1989, the sect was granted legal recognition, but by then accusations had been made (as they have been made against other religious organizations) that members were alienated from their families. A Yokohama lawyer, Sakamoto Tsutsumi, began to investigate, but in November 1989, he, his wife, and their infant son disappeared and their bodies were not discovered until September 1995.

Asahara announced the coming **Armageddon**, and his followers began to build nuclear shelters. At the same time, he ordered the manufacture of sarin gas. On June 27, 1994, clouds of sarin killed seven people and affected hundreds in a district of Matsumoto in central Japan, where a tribunal of judges was set to hear a case against Aum Shinrikyo. It was not until January 1995 that the connection with the sect was established, and on March 19, 1995, police raided the sect's headquarters in Osaka. It was the

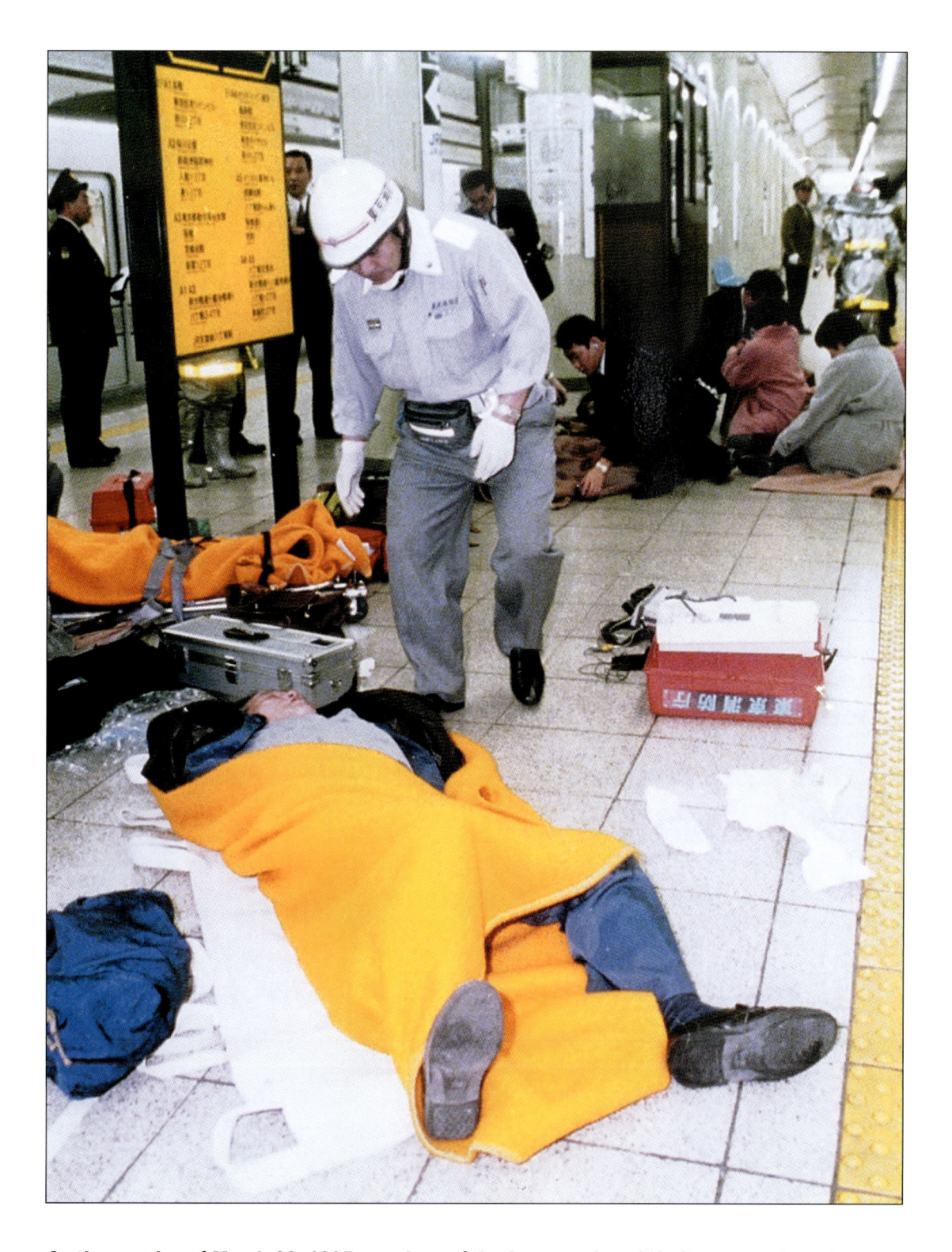

On the morning of March 20, 1995, members of the Japanese Aum Shinrikyo sect released containers of the nerve gas sarin in the commuter-crowded subway system of Tokyo. Thousands of people were seriously incapacitated, and 12 died. The leader of the sect, together with his 104 followers, were later indicted for the crime.

68   INTERNATIONAL TERRORISM

Timothy McVeigh, who exploded a bomb at the Alfred P. Murrah Federal Building in Oklahoma City in April 1995, claimed the attack was carried out in revenge for the deaths of Branch Davidians at Waco, Texas, in 1993. As this photograph of a demonstrator outside Terre Haute Penitentiary, Indiana, shows, some citizens applauded his action.

next morning that the subway attack took place in Tokyo. There followed an assassination attempt against the head of the National Police Agency and further gas attacks on trains, fortunately with no deaths.

Asahara was found in hiding, and he and 104 followers were indicted for their crimes. Aum Shinrikyo, however, survives, after changing its name to Aleph—but they have not renounced their former leader. As their new leader, Fumihiro Joyu, told *The New York Times*: "Just like you wouldn't stop your connection with physical fathers and mothers who commit a crime, we will not sever our connections with our spiritual father."

AMERICAN CHRISTIAN TERRORISTS

The association of Christian extremism with violence has recently become a worrying factor in the United States. Whether the Branch-Davidian sect, many of whom died resisting a siege by the ATF and FBI at Waco, Texas, in 1993, could be considered terrorists is open to question. But when Timothy McVeigh and Terry Nichols built a bomb to destroy the Alfred P. Murrah Federal Building in Oklahoma City in 1995, their motive was announced as revenge for the Waco deaths.

McVeigh was a follower of the armed "citizens' militias," of which there are estimated to be some 800, with a claimed membership of five million. They are closely associated with the Christian Patriots, who are obsessed with the religious and racial "purification" of the United States and advocate the overthrow of the government to attain this goal. One militia recruit described his induction in a rural Missouri church:

"It was extremely religious. There were people standing along the aisles carrying weapons, rifles, and a few with pistols. We all stood up and walked to the front of the church in this strange procession. We were told that it was part of the ritual of becoming 'God's soldiers' in this 'holy war.' One of the organizers of the event then mounted the pulpit, declaring 'Soon we will be asked to kill, but we will kill with love in our hearts because God is with us.'"

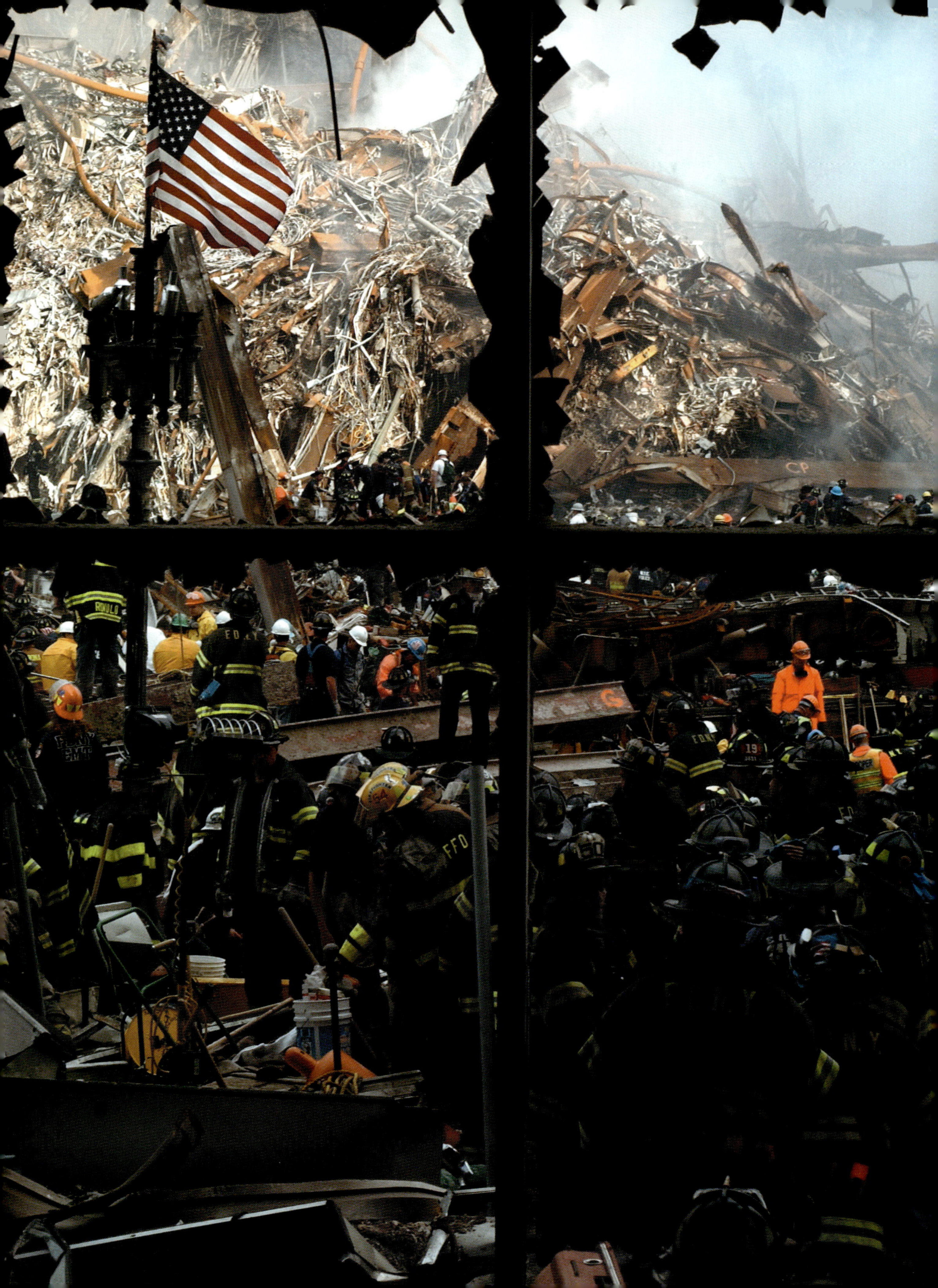
CP

Osama bin Laden and Al Qaeda

Some years before the destruction of the twin towers of the World Trade Center in New York City on September 11, 2001, Osama bin Laden was already named by the press "the most wanted man in the world."

Osama was born in Riyadh, the capital of Saudi Arabia, in 1957, a son of one of the richest industrialists in the Middle East, Mohammad bin Oud bin Laden. Mohammad was a Yemeni, who moved to Saudi Arabia when Abdelaziz Ibn Saud established it as a kingdom in 1932. A construction engineer, he gradually built up his business, eventually securing the contract to build the royal palace in Jiddah. From that time on, he became intimate with the royal family and, it is said, played a part in securing the succession of King Faisal to the throne in 1964. His construction company flourished, responsible for most of the buildings, not only in Saudi Arabia, but also in Kuwait and Beirut: in the mid-1990s, the company's worth was estimated at $36 billion. When he died in a plane crash in the early 1970s, Faisal is reported to have said, "Today I have lost my right arm."

OSAMA'S EARLY LIFE

Osama was the 17th son among 52 sons and daughters fathered by Mohammad. Although his father was a devout Muslim, Osama led a life as a young man that was incompatible with strict Islamic standards, paying

Left: September 11, 2001, like the Japanese attack on Pearl Harbor in December 1941, will go down in American history as "a day of infamy." Here, as the Stars and Stripes flies from a lamp-post, New York City firemen begin the task of sifting through the devastation of the Twin Towers.

frequent visits to Beirut in Lebanon. "Those who knew him when he was in Beirut," it has been alleged, "all said the same thing. He was spreading cash in clubs and bars. He drank quantities of alcohol, a binge-drinker, and he had an eye for the ladies."

Nevertheless, after marrying a distantly related Syrian girl, bin Laden chose to study civil engineering, not abroad (as many of his brothers had chosen), but at the university in Jiddah, where he was gradually transformed into an Islamic hard-liner. At the same time, he became increasingly resentful of the prominence of his elder half-brothers, particularly rich playboy Salim—who was killed in 1985, when he flew his hang glider into power lines in Texas. Much later, a 1998 article in the *St. Louis Post-Dispatch* described a meeting at this time with bin Laden:

"Clean-shaven and soft-spoken, Osama was dressed in a well-tailored Western suit and tie. There was no mistaking the unease with which Osama regarded his elder half-brother. After our brief introduction, Salim dismissed Osama with a wave of his hand, and the young man backed away with a look of cold frustration in his eyes."

Upon his father's death, Osama is said to have received, like his brothers, a vast sum, reported at over $300 million. He made the acquaintance of Prince Turki Ibn Faisal Ibn Abdelaziz, the head of the Saudi secret service, and the two became friends. When Soviet troops invaded Afghanistan on December 26, 1979, Prince Turki suggested to bin Laden that he use his wealth to establish a network of Muslim fighters to aid the Mujaheddin, who were opposing the Russians. Osama said later: "When the invasion of Afghanistan started, I was enraged and went there at once—I arrived before the end of 1979. I decided to wage jihad against Russia."

FUNDING ISLAMIC TERRORISTS

In fact, bin Laden went first to Pakistan, where he met Palestinian Abdallah Azzam, who had taught previously at the university in Jiddah. Together, they planned to train and supply **dissident** Islamists—and even to

Osama bin Laden—despite rejecting Western values—has no hesitation in exploiting the facilities of television, and has made several videotaped appearances on the Arab al-Jazeera service. The AK-47 rifle he poses with was allegedly taken from the body of a Russian general in Afghanistan.

Despite the misspelling—"Osama is our herrow"—there is no mistaking the message of these Al Qaeda supporters at a wildly enthusiastic demonstration in Karachi, Pakistan. It took place in September 2001, shortly after the destruction of the World Trade Center in New York City.

recompense their families for lost income. Osama established the Islamic Salvation Foundation to handle the funds and, with Azzam, he set up the Mekhtab al-Khidemat al-Muhajeddin (MAK) as a recruiting center. The MAK has enlisted and transported thousands of Muslims from more than 35 countries to Afghanistan, and has organized training camps in both Pakistan and Afghanistan.

How effective these fighters were, and how much time bin Laden himself spent in fighting the Russians, are matters on which commentators disagree. He was certainly present at the battle of Jalalabad. John Simpson, World Affairs Editor at the BBC, has described how bin Laden wanted his film team shot as **infidels**. When the mujaheddin refused, he flew off in a rage "and threw himself onto one of the beds, beating his fists on the pillow in frustration." The AK-47 rifle with which bin Laden posed for photographs is said to be one that he personally took from the dead body of a Soviet general killed at the battle of Shaban in 1987.

U.S. support for the Mujaheddin began in 1986, when President Reagan authorized the supply of Stinger ground-to-air missiles—one source suggests as a result of a direct meeting with bin Laden. But, Osama later said, "As soon as the withdrawal of Russian forces was announced, the United States and Saudi Arabia stopped their assistance."

THE BEGINNING OF AL QAEDA

When a car bomb killed Azzam in Peshawar, Pakistan, in November 1989, Azzam's son-in-law persuaded bin Laden to provide funds for the GIA, an Islamic terrorist group based in Algeria. It was his money that was used to finance the wave of GIA bombings in Paris in 1995—and thus the international terrorist was born.

Returning to Saudi Arabia, bin Laden was disgusted with what he found. The country was like an American colony, he said: "American companies make millions in the Arab world, with which they pay taxes to their government. The United States uses that money to send $3 billion a year to Israel, which it uses to kill Palestinians!" With the assistance of a leader of Islamic Jihad, he built up the organization he named Al Qaeda ("The Base"). By the mid-1990s, the FBI and CIA identified Al Qaeda as his principal means of international terrorist operations.

The Iraqi invasion of Kuwait in August 1990, and the subsequent Gulf War, finally turned bin Laden against the Saudi ruling class, as thousands of American, British, and allied troops arrived in Saudi Arabia. When U.S. Marines remained in Dhahran after the end of the war and Navy warships patrolled the Gulf, bin Laden's rage knew no bounds. He began to support dissident Saudi groups, and attempted to smuggle in arms from Yemen.

In 1991, he was expelled from Saudi Arabia and in 1994, he was deprived of his Saudi citizenship.

Bin Laden flew in his private jet to Khartoum in the Sudan. Here, the leader of the ruling National Islamic Front party welcomed him. He bought two houses, where he established his three wives and 15 children. He enlisted the help of follower Ali Mohammed and began to bring his "Afghan Arabs" to training camps in the Sudan. It has been reported that among the hundreds he assembled there were "Tunisians, Algerians, Sudanese, Saudis, Syrians, Iraqis, Moroccans, Somalis, Ethiopians, Eritreans, Chechnyans, Bosnians, and six African Americans." He bought weapons from Iran and China—it is claimed he spent $15 million on just one shipment, which included explosives from Czechoslovakia.

ESTABLISHING A TERRORIST NETWORK

In Sudan, bin Laden also invested in profitable businesses, helping to build a new airport at Port Sudan and a 750-mile (1210-km) road between the airport and the capital. He made similar investments in Yemen, including several obscure "import-export" companies. He set up an associate in London and made contact with the Albanian Secret Service. In December 1992, bin Laden sent Al Qaeda members to explode a bomb in a hotel in Yemen where U.S. troops had been staying; the soldiers had already left, but two Austrian tourists were blown to pieces. The troops were on their way to Somalia as part of the United Nations' "Operation Restore Hope," and on October 3-4, 1993, they were caught in a vicious attack by Al Qaeda, in which 18 were killed, many more injured, and one or more helicopters (accounts vary) shot down.

By 1995, the FBI and CIA had successfully established bin Laden's involvement in these terrorist attacks, as well as the bombing of the World Trade Center, and they consulted with counterterrorist colleagues in Britain, Israel, Germany, Italy, and France. Meanwhile, the governments of Egypt, Saudi Arabia, and the U.S. put increasing pressure on Sudan, and in

U.S. Marines flew to war-stricken Somalia in December 1992 as part of the United Nations' "Operation Restore Hope." Here, a Marines doctor tends to a two-year-old suffering from malnutrition. The Marines' humanitarian mission was later viciously attacked by Al Qaeda.

April 1996, the National Islamic Front ordered him to leave the country. He chose Afghanistan, by now dominated by the Islamic fundamentalist Taliban, as his refuge, and flew into Jalalabad in a chartered freighter with his wives and 150 supporters. Within weeks, on June 25, 1996, a huge 5,000-pound truck bomb exploded close by a U.S. military housing complex in Dhahran, killing 19 and injuring many more. Bin Laden said: "When I got the news, I was very happy. This was a noble act."

For a time, less was heard of bin Laden and Al Qaeda as he made contact with other Islamic terrorist groups and built himself a headquarters tunneled into the side of a mountain above Jalalabad.

A view of the port-side damage sustained by the guided-missile destroyer USS *Cole* in the harbor at Aden, Yemen, on October 12, 2000. Two Al Qaeda suicide volunteers had rammed the ship with a small boat packed with explosives. Seventeen sailors were killed, and dozens more injured.

DECLARING WAR ON THE U.S.

Then, on February 23, 1998, bin Laden announced the International Islamic Front for Jihad against the Jews and Crusaders:

"For over seven years the United States has been occupying the lands of Islam in the holiest of places, the Arabian peninsula, plundering its riches, dictating to its rulers, humiliating its people, terrorizing its neighbors, and turning its bases in the peninsula into a spearhead through which to fight the neighboring Muslim peoples…in compliance with God's order, we issue the following *fatwa* to all Muslims: the ruling to kill the Americans and their allies—civilians and military—is an individual duty for every Muslim…this is in accordance with the words of Almighty God…."

It was effectively a declaration of war on the United States. However, lacking legislation that would have turned the U.S. into a police state, the

FBI and CIA could do little more than mount surveillance on those who were suspected of being Al Qaeda members and track their movements in other countries. Intense diplomatic efforts were made to persuade the Taliban that their international isolation would end if they handed over bin Laden, but their leaders insisted that he would remain as their "protected guest" in Afghanistan.

Bin Laden maintained "sleeper" groups in many countries, not only those under Islamic rule, but also in Europe and the U.S. The intelligence resources of most of these countries constantly monitored the activities of the suspected "sleepers," but, on the surface, they led a quiet and respectable existence.

By 1997, U.S. investigators had firm information that Al Qaeda was established in Kenya and east Africa, but knew nothing of their plans. On July 31, 1998, Mohammed al-'Owhali, briefed by bin Laden, and another man—known only as "Azzam"—made a videotape to "celebrate their coming martyrdom." And, on the morning of August 7, 1998, the two men took a bomb-truck to the back of the U.S. embassy in Nairobi, the Kenyan capital. 'Owhali threw a stun-grenade at the Kenyan guard and ran. To cover his escape, "Azzam" fired at the embassy windows before detonating the bomb and blowing himself to pieces. At least 213 people were killed and more than 4,500 injured. Minutes later, a second truck-bomb exploded outside the U.S. embassy in Dar es Salaam, Tanzania, killing 11 and injuring 85. The upper half of the truck driver struck the embassy building—the steering wheel still clutched in his hands.

"BY THE GRACE OF ALLAH, I AM ALIVE!"

President Clinton reacted swiftly. On August 27, 1998, a fusillade of 80 Tomahawk missiles was launched from U.S. warships in the Arabian Sea. Among their targets were a Sudanese factory suspected of producing nerve gas and a number of Al Qaeda camps in Afghanistan. Sadly, the factory turned out to be manufacturing medicines for human and veterinary use

ALI MOHAMMED

Mystery surrounds the activities of Ali Mohammed. Born in Egypt, he served in the Egyptian army before traveling to the United States on an exchange program, and graduated in 1981 from the Special Forces Officers' School at Fort Bragg, North Carolina. In 1985, he settled in the U.S., and in 1986, joined the U.S. Army. He was given the rank of sergeant and was posted back to Fort Bragg. What his duties were in special operations remains unclear.

In 1989, Mohammed was in New York, providing training to Muslims wishing to fight in Afghanistan, and in November that year, he received an honorable discharge from the Army. He then left for Pakistan, where he is known to have joined up with bin Laden. A year later, FBI agents raided the New Jersey home of the man who had shot Meir Kahane in New York. There they found top secret documents taken from Fort Bragg, together with notes made in Mohammed's handwriting.

and, although the camps suffered severe damage, bin Laden was not present in any of them. "By the grace of Allah, I am alive!" he announced triumphantly in a radio message to his supporters.

The missile strikes also had the unfortunate effect of hardening many moderate Muslims in support of Al Qaeda. A covert assassination attack, employing a man named Siddiq Ahmed to poison bin Laden, failed, although it resulted in his suffering severe kidney failure. The FBI and CIA went after his financial interests, and President Clinton signed an order freezing his known American assets (although many remained undetected). Throughout Europe, authorities arrested and interrogated suspected Al Qaeda members. However, CIA surveillance was unable to anticipate the suicide attack on the USS *Cole* in the harbor at Aden, Yemen, on October 12, 2000. Two Al Qaeda volunteers—Jamal al-Badawi and Taufiq al-Atash—rammed the warship with a small boat packed with explosives, ripping a 40-foot (12-m) hole in the hull and killing 17 sailors.

In 1999, a British expert wrote: "Despite the scale of his organization, the future for Osama bin Laden himself looks bleak. He cannot stay in Afghanistan forever, and Western agents and mercenaries…will eventually capture or kill him." Then came the suicide attacks of September 11, 2001, on the World Trade Center and the Pentagon, and the resulting war in Afghanistan to depose the Taliban and root out Al Qaeda. But bin Laden himself, it seemed, remained indestructible.

RAMZI YOUSEF

There is a close connection between Osama bin Laden and Ramzi Ahmed Yousef (real name Abdul Basit Karim), who masterminded the bomb attack

Fundamentalist factions in Pakistan strongly opposed the war against the Taliban in Afghanistan. Fazlur Rehman, leader of the Jamiat Ulema-i-Islam party, addresses an anti-U.S. rally, held to protest the presence of U.S. forces in areas of Pakistan bordering with Afghanistan.

on New York's World Trade Center on February 26, 1993. After the attack, Yousef escaped to Pakistan, where he attempted to assassinate Benazir Bhutto, soon to become the country's prime minister, in July 1993.

In 1994, Yousef flew to Thailand and unsuccessfully attempted a bomb attack in Bangkok. Returning to Pakistan, he led a group across the border into Iran and bombed a Shi'ite shrine. Bin Laden then asked him to travel to the Philippines to train members of the Abu Sayyaf Group in the use of explosives, with the aim of assassinating President Clinton when he visited the islands on November 12, 1994. However, Yousef decided that the security surrounding the president would be too tight and instead toyed with the idea of the Pope as an alternative target. As an experiment, he successfully exploded a time-delay bomb aboard a PAL flight from Manila to Tokyo; one passenger was killed, but the plane made a successful emergency landing in Okinawa. Eventually, Yousef returned to Pakistan, where he was captured in February 1995.

At his subsequent trial in New York City in 1996, it was stated that Yousef had intended the bomb at the World Trade Center to cause one of the twin towers to collapse and thus bring down the other. It has also been alleged that the bomb contained sodium cyanide, so that deadly cyanide gas would have been pumped into the two buildings, but fortunately, the cyanide was burned up in the explosion. However, Osama bin Laden was to have a more terrible success in 2001.

March 2, 2002: the beginning of Operation Anaconda. U.S. soldiers from the 10th Mountain Division prepare to board Chinook helicopters at Bagram Airfield, Afghanistan, on their way to attack positions believed to be held by Al Qaeda in the mountains to the south.

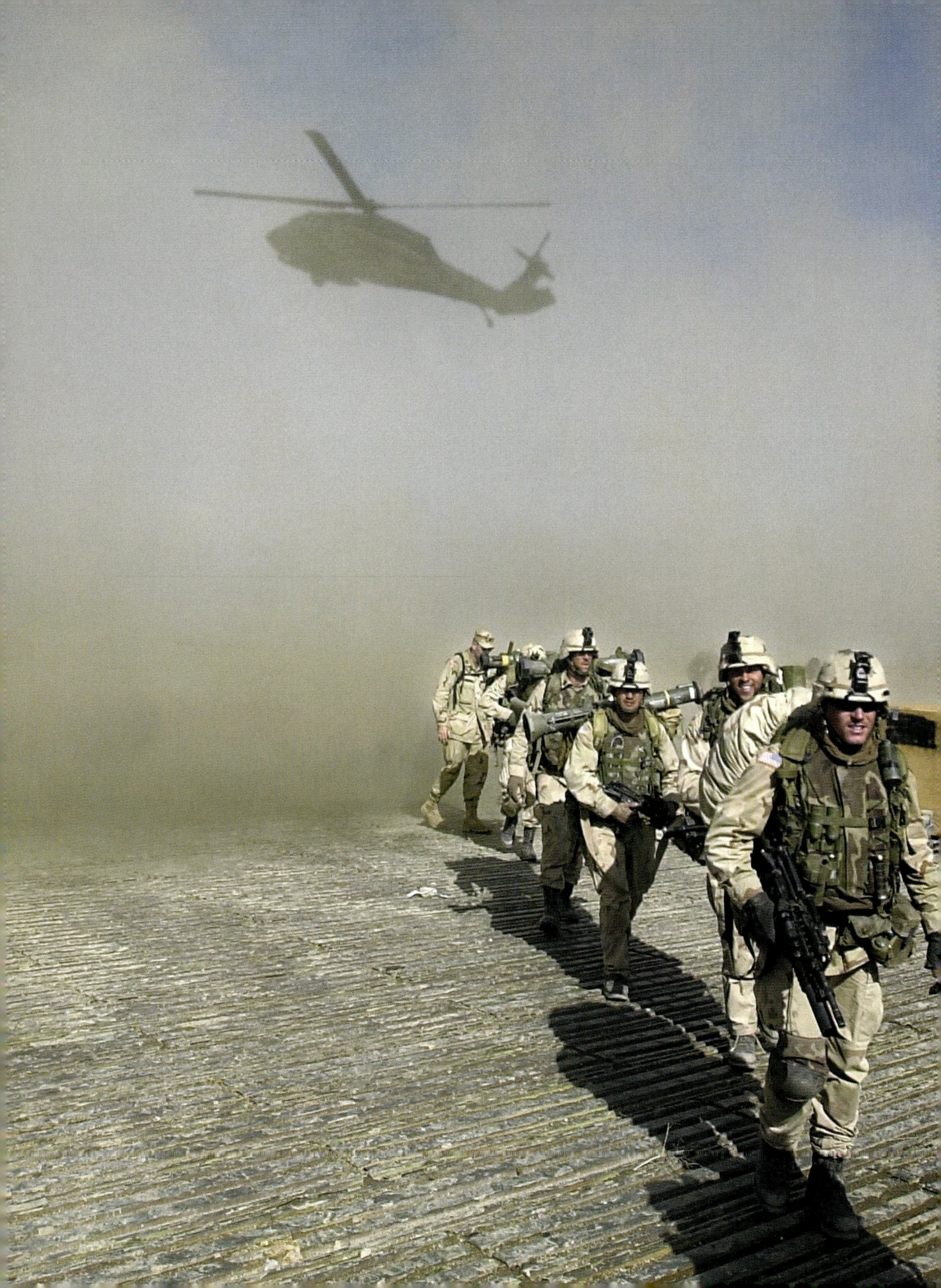

Counterterrorist Organizations

As pointed out in Chapter Two, few countries had any experience of international terrorism before the Munich Olympics massacre in 1972. Internally, states had their police organizations—both uniformed and secret—charged with detecting and arresting terrorists. However, before the foundation of Interpol, the exchange of criminal information between countries occurred only rarely, and then on an unofficial basis.

INTERNATIONAL COOPERATION

Interpol, however, exists solely to promote assistance between different national police forces and is expressly forbidden to undertake any political, military, religious, or racial functions.

The need for specific organizations devoted to the pursuit and suppression of terrorists, and willing to exchange information internationally, became urgent in 1972. It also became vitally important to study ways of dealing with **siege** situations and hostage negotiations. The failure of the West German police at Munich highlighted the problem and led to the setting up of the specialist GSG-9 (*Grenzschutzgruppe Neun*).

Other countries soon followed the German example. There are at present more than 60 specialist counterterrorist groups listed in more than 40 countries throughout the world—not counting the secret intelligence services maintained by each.

Left: Here, U.S. troops are landed in Bagram Airfield, disembarking in a cloud of dust thrown up by the rotors of their Chinook helicopters, after an abortive attempt to locate and destroy Al Qaeda groups in the mountains of Afghanistan.

It is essential that these groups be armed in any confrontation with terrorists. In some countries, units have been set up specifically for this within the national police organization, and in others, they are units of the armed forces. In Britain, for example, where the police are not normally armed (although there are special "armed response groups" held in readiness, principally for dealing with civil criminals), the Special Air Service regiment (SAS) maintains a counterrevolutionary warfare detachment, which is also deployed in Australia and New Zealand. This detachment secured a striking success in 1980, when—live on television—members stormed the Iranian embassy in London, in which 21 people were held hostage, rescuing 19 (two died during the operation) and killing five of the six terrorists.

SECRET ANTITERRORIST UNITS

In the U.S., the secretive Delta Force has the task of dealing with hostage rescue, barricade operations, and specialized reconnaissance. It was founded by Colonel C.A. Beckwith and modeled on his experience with the SAS in the 1960s. Delta Force operates out of the Special Forces establishment at Fort Bragg, North Carolina, and is made up of volunteers, principally from the 82nd Airborne, the Green Berets, and the Rangers. They are said to be the world's experts in close-quarters fighting. Although their operations are classified, it is known that they took part in the failed attempt to rescue the American hostages from the U.S. embassy in Tehran in April 1980.

Another classified unit is the U.S. Navy's SEAL Team 6 (now officially known as DevGroup), which is responsible for counterterrorist operations on water. Among their acknowledged operations have been the arrest of General Noriega in Panama in 1990 and the rescue of deposed president Jean-Bertrand Aristide from Haiti in 1991.

There is also the 160th Special Operations Aviation Regiment, known as the "Night Stalkers." Since 1987, all U.S. military counterterrorist groups have been gathered under the umbrella of USSOCOM (United

Britain's Special Air Service regiment (SAS) maintains counterrevolutionary warfare units for action against international terrorists. These men are equipped with Heckler & Koch machine pistols, climbing ropes, gas and stun grenades, gas masks, knives, and automatic handguns.

States Special Operations Command), based at MacDill, Florida.

France has several organizations, principal among which is GIGN. These are special units within the *gendarmerie,* who act as police outside major towns and cities, but are controlled by the Ministry of Defense. Another organization is the COS (*Commandement des opérations spéciales*), a military group drawn from a wide range of specialties.

By far, the longest-established counterterrorist group is the *Sareyet Mat'kal* of Israel, which was created in 1957 in the face of increasing attacks by Arabs. It was in combat with the Japanese Red Army at Lod Airport in 1972, and played a part in the successful release of 110 passengers from an Air France plane hijacked to Entebbe, Uganda, in 1976.

88 INTERNATIONAL TERRORISM

In December 1994, members of the fundamentalist Algerian GIA hijacked an Air France Airbus, planning to fly it from Marseille Airport and explode it over Paris. A unit of the French GIGN anti-terrorist organization stormed the plane, and the passengers were escorted to safety.

CIVILIAN GROUPS

All these units are essentially military organizations, but every country has civilian bureaus devoted to monitoring the activities of terrorists and securing their arrest or, in some cases, their covert assassination. In Britain, the Secret Intelligence Service (usually known as MI6) gathers intelligence on all foreign movements, while MI5 is concerned with internal threats. MI5 has no powers of arrest, which are the responsibility of probably the oldest antiterrorist force in the world, the Special Branch of the Metropolitan Police. This was originally set up in the latter 19th century as the Special Irish Branch to deal with the activities of Irish revolutionaries.

As explained in Chapter 2, the United States did not immediately follow the example of European nations, who established elite counterterrorist organizations in the aftermath of Munich 1972. The situation has changed dramatically over the years, and June 2002 saw the setting up of the

COUNTERTERRORIST ORGANIZATIONS 89

Department of Homeland Security, the first new Cabinet-level department in over 10 years. Previously, the CIA had set up a Counterterrorism Center at their Langley, Virginia, headquarters, with specialist personnel drawn from Intelligence, Operations, and Science & Technology, who briefed the White House's own Counterterrorism Security Group (CSG). The CIA also maintains a paramilitary unit, known as Special Activities Staff (SAS).

The FBI has established special Rapid Assessment and Initial Reaction (RAID) teams across the United States to deal with any chemical or biological attack, as well as an elite Hostage Rescue Team (HRT). The FBI pursues inquiries, together with the Immigration Service, the Secret Service, and police forces, to identify and arrest those suspected of terrorist affiliations. Finally, the National Security Agency at Fort George Meade, Maryland, maintains intensive monitoring of terrorist telephone, radio, and Internet communications.

However, there is one thing that remains certain. Whatever setbacks these counterterrorist organizations throughout the world suffer, and no matter how the violence of terrorists may escalate, terrorism can never, ever, succeed in the achievement of its aims.

The FBI maintains a Hostage Rescue Team (HRT) based at their headquarters in Quantico, Virginia. Here, armed agents go through their training.

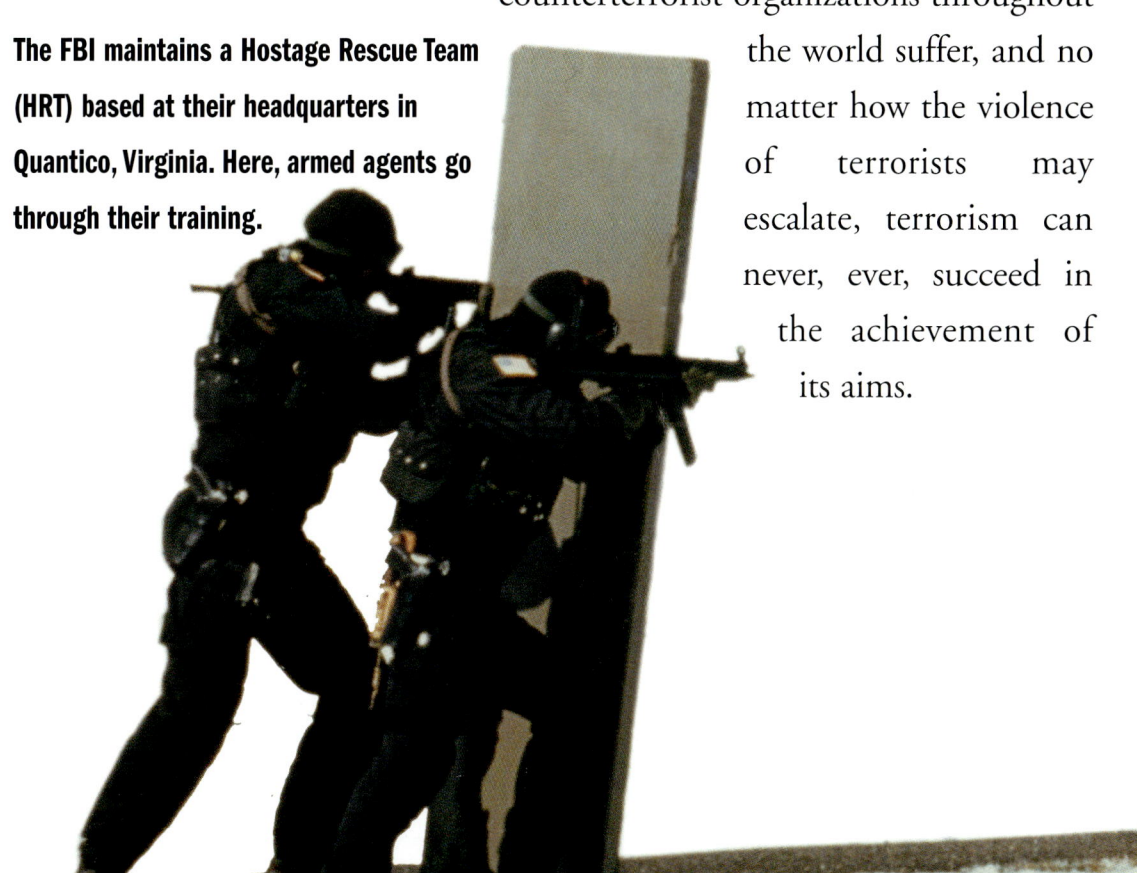

GLOSSARY

Acquittal: a setting free from the charge of an offense by verdict, sentence, or other legal process

Anarchist: strictly speaking, an anarchist believes that all forms of government are unnecessary and could be replaced by voluntary cooperation; in the popular vocabulary, however, the word came to mean someone who attacked the ruling government by means of terrorist activities

Armageddon: final battle between the forces of good and evil prophesied in Revelation, in the Bible, as the end of the world

Asylum: protection from arrest and extradition given especially to political refugees by a nation or by an embassy or other agency enjoying diplomatic immunity

Brainwash: a forcible indoctrination to induce someone to give up basic political, social, or religious beliefs and attitudes and to accept contrasting regimented ideas

Cease-fire: a suspension of active hostilities

Commune: a community characterized by collective ownership and use of property

Czar: a ruler of Russia until the 1917 revolution

Dissident: someone who disagrees with an established religious or political system, organization, or belief

Fascist: someone who supports a political philosophy that exalts nation and often race above the individual and that stands for a centralized autocratic government headed by a dictatorial leader, severe economic and social regimentation, and forcible suppression of opposition

Guerrilla: Spanish word meaning a member of an irregular military unit—that is, not one of the regular (uniformed) army

Infidel: an unbeliever with respect to a particular religion

Interpol: an association of national police forces that promotes cooperation and mutual assistance in apprehending international criminals and criminals who flee abroad to avoid justice

Manifesto: a written statement declaring publicly the intentions, motives, or views of its issuer

Martyrdom: the suffering of death on account of adherence to a cause and especially to one's religious faith

Mercenary: a man or woman who is paid by a foreign government or organization to fight in its service

Mullah: Islamic religious teacher

Republican: a person who supports a government in which supreme power resides in a body of citizens entitled to vote and is exercised by elected officers and representatives responsible to them and governing according to law

Sanction: an economic or military coercive measure adopted for forcing a nation violating international law to desist or yield to adjudication

Semite: member of a people of Caucasian stock, chiefly comprising Jews and Arabs

Shi'a: one of the two principal sects of Islam (the other is the Sunni); both adhere to the teachings of the Koran, but the Shi'a believe that the true line of succession from the prophet Muhammad descends from Ali, his cousin and brother-in-law, through succeeding "imams"

Siege (n.): a stand-off situation, in which a group holds a position by force and refuses to surrender

Ulster: one of the four ancient provinces of Ireland; in 1921, with the division of Ireland, six of the nine counties of the province were retained in the United Kingdom as Northern Ireland, which is now popularly known as Ulster

Zionism: movement dedicated to the return of the Jewish people from the Diaspora (mass exodus of the Jews) and the reestablishment of a Jewish homeland (Israel) in Palestine

CHRONOLOGY

1793:	The term "terrorist" is first used in the aftermath of the French Revolution.
1881:	Assassination of Czar Alexander II by *Narodnaya Vodya*.
1901:	Assassination of U.S. President William McKinley.
1914:	Archduke Ferdinand is assassinated in Sarajevo.
1917:	The Irish Republican Army (IRA) is formed.
1921:	Partition of Ireland proposed; cease-fire in 1923.
1948:	State of Israel founded; first Arab-Israeli war.
1956:	Arafat founds al-Fatah.
1959:	Formation of ETA in Spain.
1964:	Formation of Palestine Liberation Organization (PLO).
1966:	Formation of Black Panther Party.
1968:	PLO-related terrorists hijack El Al airliner; ETA opens terrorist campaign in Spain.
1969:	Provisional IRA ("Provos") forms in Northern Ireland; Yasser Arafat becomes chairman of PLO; Weathermen "Days of Rage" in Chicago.
1970:	PLO hijacks five airliners; Red Brigades form in Italy; Red Army Faction is formed in Germany; Japanese Red Army is formed.
1972:	Red Army Faction bombs U.S. officers' mess in Frankfurt; Black September massacres Israeli athletes at Munich Olympic Games; Japanese Red Army massacre at Lod Airport.
1973:	Red Brigades capture grandson of Paul Getty; formation of Symbionese Liberation Army in San Francisco Bay area.
1974:	Patricia Hearst is kidnapped; Yasser Arafat is invited to address UN assembly.
1975:	Carlos "the Jackal" leads attack on OPEC ministers meeting in Vienna.
1978:	Trial of Red Brigades members opens; Aldo Moro is assassinated in Rome; Direct Action is formed in France.
1979:	Earl Mountbatten is killed by Provos; Iranian revolutionaries occupy U.S. embassy in Tehran and take 52 hostages.
1981:	Red Brigades kidnaps Brigadier General James Dozier; Islamic Jihad assassinates Egyptian president Anwar Sadat.
1983:	Hezbollah bombs U.S. embassy and Marine barracks in Beirut.

1985:	Joint RAF–Direct Action attack on USAF base, Frankfurt; Palestine Liberation Front members seize *Achille Lauro* liner and murder Leon Klinghofer.
1987:	Hamas is formed in Palestine; Aum Shinrikyo is founded in Japan.
1988:	Japanese Red Army bombs U.S. officer's club in Naples, Italy; destruction of PanAm Flight 103 in air over Scotland.
1991:	Gulf War against Iraq; Osama bin Laden activates Al Qaeda; Abu Sayyaf group is formed in Philippines.
1992:	Al Qaeda explodes bomb in Yemen.
1993:	Bombing of World Trade Center, New York; Oslo Peace Accord; Al Qaeda attack "Operation Restore Hope" in Somalia.
1994:	Carlos "the Jackal" is seized; Baruch Goldstein murders 29 Palestinians in mosque; HUA kidnaps U.S. nationals in New Delhi, India; Yousef explodes bomb aboard PAL airliner.
1995:	Yousef is arrested in Pakistan and extradited to trial in United States; ETA assassination attempt on Jose Aznar; Aum Shinrikyo sarin gas attack in Tokyo subway; Yitzak Rabin is assassinated in Israel by a member of Meir Kahane; Al-Gama attempts assassination of Egyptian president Hosni Mubarak; bombing of Alfred P. Murrah Federal Building in Oklahoma City.
1996:	Al Qaeda bombing in Dhahran.
1997:	Al-Gama attacks tourists in Egypt.
1998:	Osama bin Laden announces international jihad; Good Friday agreement signed in Ireland; Al Qaeda explodes truck bombs at U.S. embassies in Nairobi and Dar-es-Salam; President Clinton authorizes missile attacks against Al Qaeda installations.
2000:	Shigenobu, founder of JRA, is arrested; Abu Sayyaf group kidnaps 30 in Philippines.
2001:	World Trade Center is destroyed by Al Qaeda terrorists and Pentagon is damaged; war declared on terrorism; HUA attack on Indian parliament.
2002:	Journalist Daniel Pearl is kidnapped and killed in Pakistan; Red Brigades claims responsibility for the assassination of Marco Biagi in Italy; Israeli army attacks Palestine.

FURTHER INFORMATION

Useful Web Sites

www.terrorism.com

www.usinfo.state.gov/topical/pol/terrrorism

www.ict.org.il

www.fas.org/irp/threat/terrorism.htm

www.terrorism.net

www.emergency.com/cntrterr.htm

www.cdi.org/terrorism

www.cia.gov/terrorism

www.usis.usemb.se/terror

www.fbi.gov/publications/terror/terroris.htm

Further Reading

Adams, James. *The Financing of Terror.* New York: Simon & Schuster, 1986.

Alpert, Jane. *Growing Up Underground.* New York: William Morrow, 1981.

Aust, Stefan. *The Baader-Meinhof Group.* London: Bodley Head, 1987.

Carr, Caleb. *The Lessons of Terror.* New York: Random House, 2002.

Collins, Eamon with Mick McGovern. *Killing Rage.* London: Grant, 1997.

Corcoran, James. *Bitter Harvest.* New York: Penguin, 1995.

Dees, Morris with James Corcoran. *Gathering Storm.* New York: Harper Collins Publishers, 1996.

Dershowitz, Alan M. *Why Terrorism Works.* New Haven: Yale University Press, 2002.

Hoffman, Bruce. *Inside Terrorism*. London: Victor Gollancz, 1998.

Jaber, Hala. *Hezbollah: Born with a Vengeance*. New York: Columbia University Press, 1997.

Long, David E. *The Anatomy of Terrorism*. New York: Free Press, 1990.

Reeve, Simon. *The New Jackals*. London: Andre Deutsch, 1999.

Searle, Patrick. *Abu Nidal: A Gun for Hire*. New York: Random House, 1992.

Schweitzer, Glen E. and Carole C. Dorsch. *Superterrorism*. New York: Plenum Trade, 1998.

Wilkinson, Paul. *Terrorism versus Democracy*. London, Frank Cass Publishers, 2001.

About the Author

Dr. Brian Innes has been writing on criminal subjects since 1966, when he began work on a series that included *The Book of Pirates, The Book of Spies*, and *The Book of Outlaws*. After contributing to the weekly publication *The Unsolved*, he provided a long series on forensic science, as well as a number of feature articles for *Real Life Crimes*; and his book, *Crooks and Conmen*, was published in 1992.

He has also written *The History of Torture* (1998); *Death and the Afterlife* (1999); and *Bodies of Evidence* (2000), a detailed study of forensic science. He has also contributed commentary for a History Channel feature on punishment. A graduate scientist, Dr. Innes spent a number of years in industry as a research biochemist, and has written extensively on scientific topics, notably for the Marshall-Cavendish *Encyclopedia of Science*. He now lives, and continues his writing, in a converted watermill and former iron forge in southern France.

INDEX

Page numbers in *italics* refer to illustrations and captions

Abu Nidal Organization (ANO) 60–1
Abu Sayyaf 64, 82
Achille Lauro 61–2
Afghanistan 77, 79–81, *83*, 85
Alex Boncayao Brigade 64
Alexander II, Czar 10–11, *11*
Al Qaeda 64, *74*, 75, 76, 77, *78*, 79–81, 85
anarchists 10–14, *12*
Anderson, Terry 22
Angry Brigade 50
Arafat, Yasser 27, 32, 33, 62
Aum Shinrikyo 66–9, *67*
Azzam, Abdallah 72–4, 75

Baader, Andreas *40*, 42, *43*, 44, 45
Baader-Meinhof Gang *see* Red Army Faction
Basques *20*, 21–3, *23*
Beckwith, Colonel C.A. 86
Begin, Menachem 18
bin Laden, Osama *53*, 64, 71–81, *73*, 82, 83
Black Hand 13
Black Panthers *35*, 42, 47, *48*
Black September 28–31, *29*, 32, 45, 60
Branch Davidians *68*, 69
Brigades Internationales (BI) 44

Cagol, Margherita 35–6, 37
Carlos "the Jackal" 45–7, *46*
Christian Patriots 69
Central Intelligence Agency (CIA) 76, 79, 80–1, 89
Clinton, Bill 51, 79, 80, 82
Collins, Michael 14
counterterrorism 31–2, 85–9
Curcio, Renato 35–6, 37–8

de Valera, Eamonn 14, 15
Direct Action 45
Dozier, Brigadier General James 38

Egypt 26, *27*, 31, 59–60
Ensslin, Gudrun *40*, *43*, 44
Euskadi Ta Askatasuna (ETA) *20*, 21–3, *23*

Fadlallah, Muhammad Hussein 22, 54–5
fascists 15, 18, 21
al-Fatah *25*, 33
Federal Bureau of Investigation (FBI) 76, 79, 80, 89, *89*
Ferdinand, Archduke 13

Foster, Dr. Marcus 49
France 31, 43–5, 87
French Revolution *9*, 10

Germany 18, 28–31, *40*, 41–3, 44
Getty, John Paul III 37
GIGN 31, 87, *88*
Goldstein, Baruch 66
GSG-9 31, *41*, 85
Gulf War 43, 59

Hamas 55, 62
Harakat ul-Ansar (HUA) 62–3
Hearst, Patricia 50–1, *51*
hijacking 26–7, *30*, 31, *32*, *41*, 42, 49, 61–2, 87, *88*
Hizballah 22, *32*, 54, *58*, 59, *60*
Hunt, Leamon 38

International Islamic Front for Jihad 78
Interpol 85–6
Iran 55–9
Irgun 18
Irish Republican Army (IRA) 14–17
Islam 53, 54–64, 71–83
    fundamentalism 56
Islamic Jihad 59–60, 75
Israel 18, 26–33, *30*, *32*, 54–5, 59, 61, 87
Italy 15, 18, 35–8, *39*

Jamaat ul-Fuqra 64
Japan 66–9
Japanese Red Army 44, 49, 65, 87
Jordan 25, 26, 27, *27*, 62

Kahane, Meir 64–6, 80
Kahane Chai 64–6
Khomeini, Ayatollah Ruhollah 55–8, 59
Klein, Hans Joachim 42, *46*
Klinghofer, Leon 62

Lebanon 25, *27*, 59
Libya 65

McKinley, William 11
McVeigh, Timothy *68*, 69
Mafia 15
Meinhof, Ulrike *40*, 42, 44, 45
MI5 88
MI6 88
Mogadishu, Somalia 31, *41*, 43
Mohammed, Ali 76, 80
Moro, Aldo 37, *39*
Moro National Liberation Front 64
Mossad 55
Mubarak, Hosni 60

Mujaheddin 74, 75
Munich Olympics 28–32, *29*, 85

NAPAP (Armed Groups for Popular Self Government) 44–5
Narodnaya Volya 10–11, *11*
National Islamic Front 76, 77
nerve gas 66–9, *67*

Oklahoma City bombing *68*, 69

Pakistan 62–3
Palestine 18, 25–33, 62
Palestine Liberation Front (PLF) 61–2
Pezi, Patricio 38
Pisacane, Carlo 10, 38
Palestine Liberation Organization (PLO) 25–33, 42, 44, 59, 60
Popular Front for the Liberation of Palestine (PFLP) 26–7
Princip, Gavrilo 13

al-Qaddafi, Muammar 65

Rabin, Yitzhak 33, 53, 66
Rafshanjani, Hashemi 59
Raspe, Jan-Carl *43*
Red Army Faction (RAF) *40*, 41–3, 44, 45, *48*
Red Brigade 35–8, *36*, *39*
Rehman, Fazlur *81*
religion 53–69
Robespierre, Maximilien 9
Rowe, Colonel James 64
Russia, anarchists 10–11

Sadat, Anwar 59
Sareyet Mat'kal 87
Special Air Service (SAS) 86, *87*
Seale, Bobby *35*
Sheikh, Ahmed Omar Saeed 63
Simpson, John 74–5
Sinn Fein 14, 17
Spain 18, *20*, 21–3
Stern Gang 18, *19*, 20
suicide bombers *61*, 78, 81
Symbionese Liberation Army (SLA) 49–51, *51*
Syria 25, *27*, 61

Taliban 77, 79, 81

USS *Cole* *78*, 81

Waco, Texas *68*, 69
Weathermen 47–8
World Trade Center, New York City 70–1
World War I 13–14, 25